TEXAS INSTRUMENTS
PROFESSIONAL BUSINESS ANALYST GUIDE

Note: The calculator keystrokes and descriptions used in this book are based on the BA-55 Professional Business Analyst™ financial calculator. The facts and information included will be generally useful when working with other specially dedicated business calculators, but the keystroke sequences will only apply directly to the BA-55 Professional Business Analyst™ calculator.

This book was developed by:
Elbert B. Greynolds, Jr., Ph.D., CPA
Associate Professor of Accounting
Southern Methodist University
Kathy A. Kelly
Steven W. Smith

With contributions by:
Basil Melnyk
Stuart B. Smith
Richard F. Ward
Robert E. Whitsitt, II

**Artwork and layout were
coordinated and executed by:**
Gaither and Davy

IMPORTANT NOTICE REGARDING PROGRAMS
AND BOOK MATERIALS

Texas Instruments makes no warranty, either express or implied, including but not limited to any implied warranties of
merchantability and fitness for a particular purpose, regard-
ing these book materials and makes such materials available
solely on an "as-is" basis.

In no event shall Texas Instruments be liable to anyone for
special, collateral, incidental, or consequential damages in
connection with or arising out of the purchase or use of
these materials and the sole and exclusive liablility to Texas
Instruments, regardless of the form of action, shall not
exceed the purchase price of this book. Moreover, Texas
Instruments shall not be liable for any claim of any kind
whatsoever against the user of these programs or book
materials by any other party.

ISBN 0-89512-055-0
Copyright © 1982, Texas Instruments Incorporated

TABLE OF
CONTENTS

TABLE OF CONTENTS
(continued)

TABLE OF
CONTENTS
(continued)

TABLE OF
CONTENTS
(continued)

TABLE OF
CONTENTS
(continued)

TABLE OF CONTENTS
(continued)

TABLE OF
CONTENTS
(continued)

TABLE OF
CONTENTS
(continued)

1 INTRODUCTION

INTRODUCTION 1

Every profession has its particular "tools of the trade." In business, one of the most important tools is a device that helps you evaluate financial alternatives. That's where the *Professional Business Analyst*™ financial calculator can come in handy.

This calculator has been designed especially for you, the business person. Its special functions—financial, cash flow, and statistical—are related specifically to business applications. For example, you may have to decide whether to invest in a savings account or a capital asset. If you choose the capital asset, you may have to choose between leasing or buying the product. Although these may seem to be easy decisions at first glance, many complex calculations are involved in selecting the option which will be the most profitable for you or your company.

Time is another important factor in many decisions. By using your calculator to quickly perform the mathematical computations, you can spend more time considering all of your alternatives. In this way, your calculator can help you be a better informed decision-maker where financial matters are involved.

Using This Book

1 INTRODUCTION

This book has been designed as a "guidebook" for solving business problems. As many practical examples as possible have been included, rather than emphasizing theory and formulas. Occasionally you'll find a brief explanation included with an example when some of the terminology or the solution procedure in the example needs additional clarification. Appendix A lists the formulas used in the cash flow, financial, and statistical calculations and in the conversion routines and specialized financial models, such as Economic Order Quantity (EOQ).

Each example includes three columns of information: Procedure, Press, and Display. The Procedure column gives a generalized description of the method used to solve the problem. The Press column illustrates the keystroke sequence, and the Display column shows you the results which appear in your calculator's display.

Each application in this book has a task-oriented heading. To find the application which you need, follow this procedure:

1. Decide the type of problem you need to solve by considering the information you have and the information you need.
2. Look in the Table of Contents and find the heading which most closely resembles the type of problem you want to solve.
3. After locating an appropriate example, follow the step-by-step keystroke sequence and enter your values instead of ours.

If you have questions about any of the calculator's functions, the following sections describe them in detail.

INTRODUCTION 1

The following features make your calculator easier to use and allow you to better realize its full potential:

Easy-to-read Liquid Crystal Display (LCD)

Constant Memory™

Even when your calculator is turned off, the Constant Memory feature saves the memory content, the mode, and all values entered in the same mode (finance, cash flow, or statistics) prior to turning the calculator off. Normal clearing functions are in effect when the calculator is turned on again. For example, pressing 2nd **Mode** clears all data entered in the previous mode, or pressing 2nd **CLmode** clears the mode registers.

IMPORTANT: The Constant Memory feature is not maintained if the batteries are discharged or removed.

APD™ Automatic Power Down

If no keys are pressed for a period of about 15 to 35 minutes, the APD feature causes your calculator to turn off automatically. When this happens, any pending calculation is lost. Press ON/C to turn the calculator on again. (The Constant Memory feature functions in the same way as when OFF is pressed.)

Display Indicator

The display of your calculator contains several indicators which are displayed when you are using the following functions and features. "STAT" indicates statistical mode. "FIN" indicates financial mode. "ANN" appears in the display each time the payment register is not equal to zero. "CF" indicates cash flow mode. "2ND" indicates that the second function of a key is being used. "K" indicates that the constant feature is on. "FIX" indicates that the decimal point is fixed to a specified number of places rather than floating. "RUN" appears each time a calculator program is running. "TRACE" indicates that the calculator's special trace feature has been selected. "MEM" appears when the calculator is in "FIN" or "STAT" mode. Displayed above "MEM" is the number of memories available for your use.

Extended Display Range (Scientific Notation)

The normal display range of your calculator is between 0.0000001 and 99999999 (positive or negative). If a result is smaller or larger than the normal display range, the calculator automatically switches the display into scientific notation. In scientific notation, the display value splits into two fields: the mantissa and the power-of-ten exponent. For example, the result of the calculation:

$$- 0.0036089 \boxed{\div} \ 10000000 \boxed{=}$$

is expressed as -3.6089×10^{-10} by your calculator. The calculator display shows:

$$-3.6089 - 10$$

In scientific notation, a positive exponent indicates how many places the decimal point should be shifted to the right. If the exponent is negative, the decimal should be moved to the left. In the last example, move the decimal point 10 places to the left to obtain the result in normal form:

   $- 0.00000000036090$

   10 places left

To become more familiar with your Professional Business Analyst™ calculator, read this section completely. It explains the basic features of the calculator, as well as the function of each key. For practice using the keys, work some of the examples in the remaining chapters of the book.

Basic Operation Keys

On and Off Keys

[ON/c]—If the calculator is OFF, pressing [ON/c] once turns the calculator on. The first time you turn on the calculator, or after you replace the batteries, clear the calculator completely by pressing [ON/c][ON/c], [2nd] **CLmode**, [2nd] **CLmem**, [2nd] **Fix** 8.

The [ON/c] key also functions as a clearing key. Pressing [ON/c] once, before any function or operation key is pressed, clears the last number you entered into the calculator. If [ON/c] is pressed after a function or operation key (including the [=] key), the display, constant, and any pending calculation are cleared.

Pressing [ON/c] twice clears the display, constant, and any pending calculation. This does not affect the memory and mode registers.

[OFF]—This key turns the calculator off and clears any uncompleted operation.

Second Function Key

Your calculator has many features to make calculations easy and accurate. To allow you access to all of these features without overloading the keyboard, many of the calculator keys have more than one function.

The first function is printed on the key. To use the first function, just press the key. The second function of a key is printed directly above it. To use a second function, press the [2nd] key (the "2ND" indicator appears in the display), and then press the function key. When [2nd] is pressed twice, the calculator performs the first function operation.

In this book, second function keys are shown in bold type. For instance, to use the second function clear memories, press [2nd] **CLmem**.

A Look At The Keys

Number Entry Keys

Numbers are entered into the calculator with the entry keys ⓪ through ⑨, ⊙, ⊞, and ⓧⓨ. As you enter any number, the decimal point is assumed (but not displayed) to the right of your entry until the decimal point key is pressed. After pressing the decimal key ⊙, the fractional part of the number is keyed in, and the decimal point "floats" to the left with it. To change the sign of a number in the display, press the change sign key ⊞ once. Pressing ⊞ a second time changes the sign back again. The x exchange y key ⓧⓨ exchanges the displayed number with the contents of the y register. This key is used to exchange divisor and dividend in division problems and to enter data and display results in certain financial and statistical calculations.

Fixed Decimal Key

This key sets a fixed number of digits to the right of the decimal point. Press ⟨2nd⟩ **Fix** and then a number key ⓪ through ⑦ corresponding to the number of decimal places you want to the right of the decimal point. Press ⟨2nd⟩ **Fix** 8 or ⟨2nd⟩ **Fix** 9 to return to a floating decimal display.

Using a fixed-decimal display does not affect the accuracy of your calculations. The calculator uses all of the internal digits (up to 11) for subsequent calculations. For example, if ⟨2nd⟩ **Fix** 2 is selected and an actual result is 6.158, the calculator displays the rounded value of 6.16 as the result. However, the calculator internally carries the actual 6.158 value to the subsequent calculation or memory (if used).

Arithmetic Keys

Basic arithmetic is handled with five operation keys: ⊞, ⊟, ⊠, ⊡, and ⊜. Each time you press an operation key, including ⟨2nd⟩ Δ% and ⟨2nd⟩ yˣ, the previous operation is completed. All of the basic operation keys can be used in any of the three modes—cash flow, financial, and statistical.

⊞—the Add Key adds the next number you enter to the number displayed.

⊟—the Subtract Key subtracts the next number you enter from the number displayed.

⏣—the Multiply Key multiplies the displayed number by the next number you enter. The displayed value must be less than 1×10^{99} or an error condition may result.

⏣—the Divide Key divides the displayed number by the next number you enter.

⏣—the Equals Key completes all previously entered operations. This key is used to obtain both intermediate and final results.

Entry errors can be corrected easily by pressing the correct arithmetic function, 2nd y^x, or 2nd Δ% key immediately after the incorrect function, or by using the clear-entry function of the ON/C key.

Example: Calculate $6 \times 7 + 3 = 45$.

Procedure	Press	Display
1. Clear calculator and select floating decimal mode.	ON/C 2nd **Fix** 8	0
2. Enter 6 + ; change + to x.	6 ⏣⏣	6
3. Enter 7 − ; change − to +.	7 ⏣⏣	42
4. Enter 4.	4	4
5. Change 4 to 3.	ON/C 3	3
6. Calculate result.	⏣	45

Algebraic Keys

Square, Square Root, and Reciprocal Keys

All three keys act immediately on the number in the display (called x), and do not affect the calculations in progress.

2nd x^2—the Square Key multiplies the number (x) in the display by itself and displays the result.

√x̄—the Square Root Key finds the number that when multiplied by itself gives you the displayed number (x) back. (x cannot be negative).

¹/x—the Reciprocal Key divides the displayed number (x) into one. (x cannot be zero.)

A Look At The Keys

Universal Power Key

y^x—this key allows you to raise a positive number to a power. To use this key:
1. Enter the number (y) you want to raise to a power.
2. Press [2nd] y^x.
3. Enter the power (x).
4. Press [=] (or any basic operation key).

To take the "xth" root of any number y ($\sqrt[x]{y}$):
1. Enter the number (y) whose root you want to find.
2. Press [2nd] y^x.
3. Enter the root (x).
4. Press [1/x].
5. Press [=] (or any basic operation key).

In either case, the variable y must be a positive number. Also, attempting to take the 0th root of a number results in an error condition.

Example: Find 2^3.

Procedure	Press	Display
1. Clear calculator and select floating decimal mode.	[ON/C][2nd] **Fix** 8	0
2. Enter y.	2 [2nd] y^x	2
3. Enter x.	3	3
4. Calculate result.	[=]	8

Logarithm Keys

[2nd] **lnx**—the Natural Logarithm Key displays the natural logarithm (base e) of the number (x) in the display. (x cannot be negative or zero.)

[2nd] **e^x**—the Natural Antilogarithm Key (e to the power x key) calculates the natural antilogarithm (base e) of the number (x) in the display.

Both of these keys act immediately on the number in the display and do not affect calculations in progress.

Example: Find the natural logarithm of 1.2 and the natural antilogarithm of 1.25.

Procedure	Press	Display
1. Clear calculator and select floating decimal mode.	[ON/c][2nd] **Fix** 8	**0**
2. Calculate logarithm of 1.2.	1.2 [2nd] **lnx**	**0.1823216**
3. Compute antilogarithm of 1.25.	1.25 [2nd] **e^x**	**3.490343**

Percent and Percent Change Keys

[%]—the Percent Key converts the number in the display to a decimal percent (divides by 100). The symbol % means percent, which is "one hundredth." The term 75% is equivalent to 75/100 or .75.

The [%] key may be used in combinations with an operation key ([+], [−], [×], or [÷]) to allow mark up, mark down, and other percentage problems to be solved easily.

   [+] n [%][=]—adds n% to the original number displayed.

   [−] n [%][=]—subtracts n% from the original number displayed.

   [×] n [%][=]—multiplies the original number in the display by n%.

   [÷] n [%][=]—divides the original number in the display by n%.

1 INTRODUCTION

$\boxed{\text{2nd}}$ Δ%—the Percent Change (or "Delta Percent") Key calculates the percent change between two values x_1 and x_2, where:

$$\Delta\% = \frac{x_1 - x_2}{x_2} \times 100$$

Example: Suppose you keep track of the mileage you get from your car, and for a while you've been getting 17.0 miles per gallon. You have your car tuned up, and the mileage jumps to 19.8 MPG. What's the percent increase?

Procedure	Press	Display
1. Clear calculator and select floating decimal mode.	$\boxed{\text{ON/c}}$ $\boxed{\text{2nd}}$ **Fix** 8	0
2. Enter new mileage (x_1).	19.8 $\boxed{\text{2nd}}$ Δ%	**19.8**
3. Enter old mileage (x_2).	17	**17**
4. Calculate percent change.	$\boxed{=}$	**16.470588**

Constant Key

$\boxed{\text{2nd}}$ K—this key stores a number and an operation (+, −, x, ÷, Δ%, or %) for use in repetitive calculations. Select any of the following key sequences to input a constant value (M) and a constant math operation. Then enter a new number and press $\boxed{=}$. The calculator automatically supplies the math operation and the constant value needed to complete the problem.

$\boxed{+}$ $\boxed{\text{2nd}}$ K M $\boxed{=}$—adds M to each subsequent entry.

$\boxed{-}$ $\boxed{\text{2nd}}$ K M $\boxed{=}$—subtracts M from each subsequent entry.

$\boxed{\times}$ $\boxed{\text{2nd}}$ K M $\boxed{=}$—multiplies each subsequent entry by M.

$\boxed{÷}$ $\boxed{\text{2nd}}$ K M $\boxed{=}$—divides each subsequent entry by M.

$\boxed{\text{2nd}}$ Δ% $\boxed{\text{2nd}}$ K M $\boxed{=}$—calculates the percent change (Δ%) between each subsequent entry x_1 and M, where:

$$\Delta\% = \frac{x_1 - M}{M} \times 100$$

(First entry) ⊞ 2nd K M ⌘ ⊟ —adds M% of any entry to that entry.

(First entry) ⊟ 2nd K M ⌘ ⊟ —subtracts M% of any entry from that entry.

Example: Multiply 2, 4, and 7 by 3.1416.

Procedure	Press	Display
1. Clear calculator and select floating decimal mode.	ON/C 2nd **Fix** 8	**0**
2. Enter first value.	2	**2**
3. Set constant calculation.	X 2nd K 3.1416	**3.1416**
4. Calculate result.	⊟	**6.2832**
5. Calculate second result.	4 ⊟	**12.5664**
6. Calculate third result.	7 ⊟	**21.9912**

IMPORTANT: Although you can set the constant function in all modes, there are some limitations. The constant is cleared in the financial mode when any financial computation is performed. The constant is also cleared in the statistical mode when any variable is entered. Since the constant number is stored in the y register, using ⌘ can cause erroneous results.

Memory Keys

The calculator may have a maximum of five user data memories numbered 1 through 5 while in the finance mode and three user data memories numbered 1 through 3 while in the statistics mode. There are no user data memories avaliable in the cash flow mode. The following keys and operations allow manipulations of the numbers in the user data memories.

[2nd] **CLmem**—the Clear Memories Key clears the user data memories. The display, statistical, and financial registers, and program steps are not affected. If [2nd] **CLmem** is pressed in the cash flow mode, the ten cash flows are cleared and all frequencies are set to one.

[STO] m—the Store Memory Key stores the value shown in the display in user data memory m. For instance, the key sequence 3 [STO] 1 stores the value 3 in user data memory number 1.

[RCL] m—the Recall Memory Key recalls to the display the number in user data memory m. For instance, the key sequence [RCL] 2 recalls to the display the number that was in user data memory number 2. The number that was in the display is lost.

[SUM] m—the Sum Memory Key adds the displayed value to the value in the user data memory m, without affecting any calculation in progress. Note: To ensure that the previous memory content does not affect your calculation, always use [STO] to store the first quantity of a new problem or clear the memories with [2nd] **CLmem**.

[EXC] m—the Exchange Memory Key exchanges the value in the display with the value in user data memory m.

Example: Store 5.6 in memory 2 and add 8.7. Enter 12.8 and exchange it with the result in memory 2. Recall 12.8.

If the memory indicator does not show at least one data memory available, press [2nd] **CP** before entering the solution.

Procedure	Press	Display
1. Clear calculator and mode registers; select floating decimal mode.	[ON/C] [2nd] **CLmode** [2nd] **Fix** 8	0
2. Press [2nd] **Mode** until the "FIN" indicator is displayed.	[2nd] **Mode**	0
3. Store first value.	5.6 [STO] 2	**5.6**
4. Add second value to first.	8.7 [SUM] 2	**8.7**
5. Enter third value and ex-change with result.	12.8 [EXC] 2	**14.3**
6. Recall third value.	[RCL] 2	**12.8**

Mode Keys

Your calculator operates in three different modes: finance, statistics, and cash flow. Press [2nd] **Mode** repeatedly until the appropriate indicator appears in the display: "FIN", "STAT", and "CF", respectively.

Keys which are unique to one mode do not work when the calculator is in another mode. Pressing a key unique to a mode which the calculator is not in causes "Error" to be displayed. Any data which is entered in one mode cannot be transferred to another mode.

To clear all data stored in the mode registers, press [2nd] **CLmode**. All previously entered data and intermediate results in the mode registers are also cleared by pressing [2nd] **Mode**.

A Look At The Keys

Financial Keys

Compound Interest Calculations (Single Sum)

When performing compound interest calculations, select the financial mode by pressing [2nd] **Mode** until "FIN" appears in the display. The four basic elements of compound interest computations are:

[N]—the total number of compounding periods.

[%i]—the percent interest per compounding period.

[PV]—the present value (what your money is worth today).

[FV]—the future value (what your money will be worth in the future).

Enter the three known values. Then press [CPT] and the key for the unknown value. The calculator solves the compound interest problem for you. (For compound interest calculations, the payment must be zero.)

Example: How much should you pay for an investment returning $133.10 at the end of three years if you want to earn 10% compounded annually?

Procedure	Press	Display
1. Clear the calculator and fix decimal to two places.	[ON/C] [2nd] Fix 2	0.00
2. Press [2nd] **Mode** until the "FIN" indicator is displayed.	[2nd] **Mode**	0.00
3. Enter total number of compounding periods.	3 [N]	3.00
4. Enter annual interest rate.	10 [%i]	10.00
5. Enter future value.	133.10 [FV]	133.10
6. Solve for present value.	[CPT] [PV]	100.00

Paying $100 for the future amount returns 10%. However, if you pay less than $100 for the investment, the return is higher than 10%.

Annuity Problems (Series of Equal Payments)

Your calculator recognizes an annuity calculation when [PMT] (the Payment Key) is used with the other financial keys. The calculator solves for the unknown value in ordinary annuity or annuity due computations when you enter any four of the five values. (Ordinary annuities are equal payment situations where payments are made at the end of a specified period. Annuities due occur when payments are made at the beginning of the period.) To work annuity calculations, your calculator should be in the financial mode; press [2nd] **Mode** until "FIN" appears in the display.

The basic elements of an annuity problem are:

[N]—the total number of payment periods. (Entries and results are automatically rounded to four significant digits with this key.)

[%i]—the percent interest per payment period.

[PMT]—the amount of the regular payment. ("ANN" appears in the display to indicate that the payment value for an annuity calculation is not zero.)

[PV]—the total of the PV of the equal payments and the value in the FV register.

[FV]—the total of the FV of the equal payments and the value in the PV register.

[CPT]—the key used to compute an ordinary annuity.

[2nd] **Due**—the key used to compute an annuity due.

The calculator is capable of directly solving annuity problems involving present and future value. When payments are compounded forward (future value is given or is being computed), enter the payment as a negative value. When payments are discounted back (present value is given or is being computed), enter the payment as a positive value.*

After you enter the four known values, solve for the unknown by pressing [CPT] (to compute an ordinary annuity) or [2nd] **Due** (to compute an annuity due), followed by the key for the variable you are computing.

*See Appendix A for the formula.

A Look At The Keys

INTRODUCTION

Example: The Big D Company is depositing $5,000 in a sinking fund at the end of each quarter for three years to provide for the purchase of real estate. Assuming the fund pays 16% annual interest with quarterly compounding, what is the value at the end of three years?

Procedure	Press	Display
1. Clear calculator and select two decimal places.	[ON/C] [2nd] Fix 2	0.00
2. Press [2nd] Mode until the "FIN" indicator is displayed.	[2nd] Mode [2nd] CLmode	0.00
3. Calculate and enter number of total payments.	3 [X] 4 [=] [N]	12.00
4. Enter annual interest rate and calculate periodic rate.	16 [÷] 4 [=] [%i]	4.00
5. Enter payment amount.	5000 [+/−] [PMT]	−5000.00
6. Compute future value.	[CPT] [FV]	75129.03

The Big D Company can withdraw $75,129.03 from the sinking fund at the end of three years.

IMPORTANT: The calculator clears the display of all information except the indicators while performing calculations. Keyboard entries are ignored when the display is blank. The computations of %i typically may take five to 30 seconds. If unrealistic values are entered for computation of %i, the calculating time may be minutes or even hours. If this occurs, press [OFF] once and then [ON/C] twice to go on to another calculation.

The following two key descriptions cover special amortization functions. The information that must be in place before using these functions is the percent interest ([%i]), the payment amount ([PMT]), the present value ([PV]) or loan amount, and the number of periods ([N]). Enter three variables, then compute the fourth before using the following functions.

Principal and Interest Key

[2nd] **P/I**—this key determines the principal amount of payment for a fully amortized, direct-reduction loan for any payment number entered in the display. After the principal is displayed, press [x:y] to display the amount of interest included in that payment. The calculator must be in financial mode ("FIN" shows in display) for calculations involving the [2nd] **P/I** key. For beginning of period payments, press [2nd] **Due** before [2nd] **P/I** and for end of period payments press [CPT] before [2nd] **P/I**.

Accumulated Interest and Loan Balance Keys

[2nd] **Acc** and [2nd] **Bal**—when you use these keys, the calculator must be in the financial mode ("FIN" shows in the display). The [2nd] **Acc** key finds the accumulated interest paid from the first payment through the payment number entered in the display (inclusive). Pressing the [2nd] **Bal** key displays the balance remaining on the loan principal after the specified payment. For end of period payments, press [CPT] and for beginning of period payments press [2nd] **Due** before [2nd] **Acc** and [2nd] **Bal**.

Follow this procedure to calculate the accumulated interest paid from the mth through the nth payments, inclusive:

1. Enter nth payment number, press [2nd] **Acc**, wait for result, then press [STO] j.
2. Enter mth payment number, press [2nd] **Acc**, wait for result, then press [+/-][SUM] j.
3. Press [RCL] j to display accumulated interest.

Annual Percentage Rate Key

[APR▸]—this key converts annual percentage rates to annual effective rates. Enter the number of compounding periods per year. Press [APR▸], then enter the annual percentage rate, and press [=] to calculate the annual effective rate. The calculator must be in the financial mode ("FIN" shows in display) to use this key.

Annual Effective Rate Key

⟨EFF⟩—this key converts annual effective rates to annual percentage rates. Enter the number of compounding periods per year for the annual percentage rates. Press ⟨EFF⟩, then enter the annual effective rate, and press ⟨=⟩ to calculate the annual percentage rate. The calculator must be in the financial mode ("FIN" shows in the display) to use this key.

Cash Flow Keys

In annuities, all payments are equal, periodic, and of the same nature (inflow or outflow). A more general case, however, is a series of unequal cash flows, each being either an inflow or an outflow. These unequal cash flows are usually called *Variable Cash Flows* or *Uneven Cash Flows*. Furthermore, you can have a series of cash flows that remain constant for a number of payment periods and then change to a different amount for a number of periods. Cash flows having such a pattern are often called *Grouped Cash Flows*. The calculator routine used for variable and for grouped cash flows allows you to indicate whether the cash flows occur at the end or at the beginning of each period.

You can compute the Net Present Value or the Internal Rate of Return directly on your calculator for 10 different cash flows and a time period zero cash flow, or 10 groups of cash flows from one to 999 cash flows in each group and a time period zero cash flow. Depending on the solution key sequence, cash flows can be placed at the end or the beginning of each payment period. The keys used for input and solution are:

⟨%i⟩—the Percent Interest Key enters the interest rate per cash flow period for computing the Net Present Value. In the Cash Flow mode, this key operates as an input key only.

⟨PV⟩—the Present Value Key enters the time period zero cash flow. If the cash flow is an outflow, enter the value as a negative number by pressing ⟨+/−⟩ before pressing ⟨PV⟩. In the Cash Flow mode, this key operates as an input key only.

CF [STO] m—the Cash Flow Key sequence enters the cash flow amount into the calculator. The CF represents the cash flow amount while the m represents the storage location. Cash flows 1 through 9 are entered using CF1 [STO] 1, CF2 [STO] 2,..., CF9 [STO] 9, while cash flow 10 is entered using CF10 [STO][·]. The cash flow amount cannot exceed eight digits. Any cash flow entered can be reviewed by pressing [RCL] m, e.g., [RCL] 2.

[2nd] **Frq** n—the Frequency Key sequence enters the number of sequenced cash flows for the amount of CF entered using the [STO] command. After storing the cash flow, pressing [2nd] **Frq** causes the calculator to display "FR 000". You then enter the number of sequenced cash flows and press [STO] j. The amount of the cash flow will reappear in the display. If the cash flow occurs only once, omit the frequency key sequence because the calculator automatically uses a frequency of one. To review the number of cash flows in each group, press [RCL] j [x:y].

[2nd] **NPV**—the Net Present Value Key computes the net present value for a series of uneven cash flows.

[2nd] **IRR**—the Internal Rate of Return Key computes the interest rate for a series of cash flows that makes the net present value equal to zero. This interest rate is usually called the internal rate of return. Computations using this key typically require 60 seconds or longer to complete.

When the [CPT] key is pressed before [2nd] **NPV** or [2nd] **IRR**, the calculator assumes that the cash flows, other than CF0, occur at the end of each payment period, i.e., the first cash flow occurs at the end of the first cash flow period.

When the [2nd] **Due** key is pressed before [2nd] **NPV** or [2nd] **IRR**, the calculator assumes that the cash flows occur at the beginning of each payment period, i.e., the first cash flow occurs at the beginning of the first cash flow period which is the same as time period zero. See Chapter 2 for discussion and examples of variable and grouped cash flows.

A Look At The Keys

Statistical Keys

Statistical Data Entry and Removal Keys

[Σ+]—the Sigma Plus Key enters data points for statistical calculations. After you enter a data point, the calculator displays the current total number (n) of data points entered.

[2nd] Σ− —the Sigma Minus Key removes unwanted data points from the stored data sequence. After a data point is removed, the calculator displays the current total number (n) of stored data points.

[2nd] Frq—the Frequency Key is used when several identical data points are to be entered. Enter them using the following key sequence: (data point), [2nd] Frq, (number of data points), [Σ+]. Remove identical data points with this sequence: (data point), [2nd] Frq, (number of data points), [2nd] Σ− .

The mode registers retain all entered data even after you turn off the calculator. This means you can add data points to a previously entered data sequence without having to reenter the data.

The procedure to enter and remove an array of data is provided in the following chart.

Single-Variable Data	Two-Variable Data
1. To enter single occurrence data points	
• Enter data point.	• Enter "x" data point.
• Press [Σ+].	• Press [x:y].
• Repeat for next data point.	• Enter "y" data point.
	• Press [Σ+].
	• Repeat for next data point.
2. To remove single occurrence data points entered	
• Press [ON/c][x:y].	• Enter unwanted "x" data point.
• Enter unwanted data point.	• Press [x:y].
• Press [2nd] Σ−.	• Enter unwanted "y" data point.
	• Press [2nd] Σ− .

Single-Variable Data	Two-Variable Data

3. To enter multiple occurrence data points

• Enter data point.	• Enter "x" data point.
• Press [2nd] **Frq.**	• Press [x:y].
• Enter number of repetitions.	• Enter "y" data point.
• Press [Σ+].	• Press [2nd] **Frq.**
• Repeat for next data points.	• Enter number of repetitions.
	• Press [Σ+].
	• Repeat for next data points.

4. To remove multiple occurrence data points entered

• Press [ON/c][x:y].	• Enter unwanted "x" data point.
• Enter unwanted data point.	• Press [x:y].
• Press [2nd] **Frq.**	• Enter unwanted "y" data point.
• Enter number of repetitions.	• Press [2nd] **Frq.**
• Press [2nd] **Σ−**.	• Enter number of repetitions.
	• Press [2nd] **Σ−**.

Once entered, the data is used to calculate the mean, standard deviation, and variance by pressing the appropriate keys.

IMPORTANT: Since the calculator can hold statistical data in the mode registers even when it is turned off, always clear the registers with [2nd] **CLmode** before entering a new set of statistical data.

Mean, Standard Deviation, and Variance Keys

[$\bar{y}$]—the y Mean Key gives the mean of the "y" values entered.

[$\bar{x}$]—the x Mean Key gives the mean of the "x" values entered.

Note that the mean keys remove any pending operations.

$\boxed{\sigma n}$, $\boxed{\sigma n}\boxed{x{:}y}$—the Population Standard Deviation Keys give the population standard deviation of the y data points and the x data points entered, respectively.

$\boxed{\sigma n\text{-}1}$, $\boxed{\sigma n\text{-}1}\boxed{x{:}y}$—the Sample Standard Deviation keys give the sample standard deviation of the y data points and the x data points entered, respectively.

The difference between the sample standard deviation (Sn − 1) and the population standard deviation (Sn) becomes very small for over 30 data points. A population is usually a large set of items, and a sample is a smaller portion selected from the population. Note that the standard deviation keys remove any pending operations.

$\boxed{\sigma n}\boxed{2nd}$ x^2—this key sequence calculates the variance of a population (with n weighting).

$\boxed{\sigma n\text{-}1}\boxed{2nd}$ x^2—this key sequence calculates the variance of a sample (with n − 1 weighting).

The various key sequences that may be used to analyze an array of statistical data are provided in the following chart.

Single-variable Data	Two-variable Data
• Enter first data point.	Call the two sets of data "x"
• Press $\boxed{\Sigma+}$.	(independent) and "y" (dependent)
• Repeat for all data points.	arrays of data.
	• Enter first "x" data point.
	• Press $\boxed{x{:}y}$.
	• Enter first "y" data point.
	• Press $\boxed{\Sigma+}$.
	• Repeat for all points.

Single-variable Data	Two-variable Data
• Press $\bar{y}$ to calculate the mean of the data.	• Press $\bar{y}$ to calculate the mean of the "y" data points. Then press $\bar{x}$ to display the mean of the "x" data points.
• Press σ_{n-1} to calculate the standard deviation of the data using n − 1 weighting (normally used for sample data).	• Press σ_{n-1} to calculate the standard deviation of the "y" data using n − 1 weighting. Then press $x{:}y$ to display the standard deviation of the "x" data using n − 1 weighting.
• Press σ_n to calculate the standard deviation of the data using n weighting.	• Press σ_n to calculate the standard deviation of the "y" data points using n weighting. Then press $x{:}y$ to display the standard deviation of the "x" data points using n weighting.
• Press σ_{n-1} $2nd$ x^2 to calculate the variance of the data (with n − 1 weighting).	• Press σ_{n-1} $2nd$ x^2 to calculate the variance of the "y" data points with n − 1 weighting. Then press $x{:}y$ to display the variance of the "x" data points with n − 1 weighting.
• Press σ_n $2nd$ x^2 to calculate the variance of the data with n weighting.	• Press σ_n $2nd$ x^2 to calculate the variance of the "y" data points with n weighting. Then press $x{:}y$ to calculate the variance of the "x" data points with n weighting.

A Look At The Keys

Example: You are teaching a course and the first set of test scores is as shown below.

  96 65 81 85 76 86 57 98 75 78 100 72 81 70 80

What are the mean and standard deviation of these scores?

Procedure	Press	Display
1. Clear the calculator and mode registers; select- floating decimal point.	ON/C 2nd CLmode 2nd Fix 8	0
2. Press 2nd Mode until the "STAT" indicator is displayed.	2nd Mode	0
3. Enter data points.	96 Σ+ 65 Σ+ 81 Σ+ 85 Σ+ 76 Σ+ 86 Σ+ 57 Σ+ 98 Σ+ 75 Σ+ 78 Σ+ 100 Σ+ 72 Σ+ 81 Σ+ 70 Σ+ 80 Σ+	15
4. Calculate mean.	ȳ	80
5. Calculate standard deviation.	σn	11.564313

Linear Regression and Trend Line Analysis

Linear regression is useful for analyzing historical data and using the results to project future information. The data points you know are entered by their "x" and,"y" coordinates using the two-variable data entry procedure described at the beginning of this section.

Trend line analysis is a variation of linear regression that's useful in making predictions based on trends or growth. In trend line analysis, the "x" values are automatically increas- ed by one for each data point. Your calculator does this for you—all you need to do is enter the first "x" value with the x:y key, and then enter consecutive "y" values with the Σ+ key. The calculator automatically increments the "x" variable by one for each "y" value you enter. If an error is made in data entry, simply press [2nd] **Σ−** to remove the incorrect entry before making another entry.

In both linear regression and trend line analysis situations, your calculator computes a straight line graph through the series of data points entered. The actual placement of the line is determined by a least-squares linear regression that minimizes the sum of the squares of the deviation of the y values from the straight line of best fit. The linear equation of the form $y = ax + b$ is determined for the line.

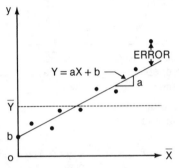

[2nd] **Intcp**—the Intercept Key calculates the y-intercept (b) of the line.

[2nd] **Slope**—the Slope Key calculates the slope (a) of the line.

[2nd] **Fcst Y**—the Forecast Key calculates the y′ value for a given x value on the calculated regression line.

[2nd] **Corr**—the Correlation Coefficient Key calculates the correlation coefficient of the data entered in the linear regression routine. This value will fall between −1 and +1. The closer the result to +1 or −1, the better the existing correlation is. A value of zero (0) means that no correlation exists between the data points.

Note: If the line is vertical, no y-intercept exists and the slope is undefinable. Calculating the slope yields an error condition and additional "x" points cannot be predicted. If the line is horizontal, the slope is 0 and new "y" values cannot be predicted.

Example: Suppose that you have been keeping records of the amount of rainfall each July in your city for the last five years. Can you use this data to predict the amount of rainfall this July? The data you have are shown below.

Year	Rainfall in centimeters
1977	8.6
1978	11.2
1979	11.0
1980	4.1
1981	5.3

Procedure	Press	Display
1. Clear the calculator and mode registers; select floating decimal.	[ON/C] [2nd] **CLmode** [2nd] **Fix** 8	0
2. Press [2nd] **Mode** until the "STAT" indicator is displayed.	[2nd] **Mode**	0
3. Enter first year and rainfall.	1977 [x:y] 8.6 [Σ+]	1
4. Enter remaining rainfall; the x value is automatically incremented.	11.2 [Σ+] 11 [Σ+] 4.1 [Σ+] 5.3 [Σ+]	5
5. Calculate correlation.	[2nd] **Corr**	− 0.6677606
6. Forecast rainfall for 1982.	1982 [2nd] **Fcst Y**	3.9299999

Programming Keys

In addition to all the preprogrammed features of the BA-55, this calculator is also programmable when in the financial mode. This means you can teach the calculator to automatically perform a variety of calculations with up to 40 steps and then have it execute these steps as often as you like with a simple key sequence. In this section, the calculator keys that are devoted to programs and programming are discussed.

The way the calculator learns a program is quite simple. There is a special memory inside called a program memory. It remembers the program keystrokes you press. As you program the calculator, each keystroke sequence is stored, in order, as a simple code. When the program is run, the calculator reads the codes and presses the keys in the exact sequence in which they were entered.

The memory of the calculator may be visualized as shown in the following diagram.

User Data Memories   0 1 2 3 4 5
                               40 32 24 16 08 00   Program steps

The user data memories are numbered 0 through 5, starting at the left of the diagram. The program steps are numbered 00 through 40, starting at the right of the diagram. Each user data memory takes up the room for eight program steps.

The calculator automatically partitions for additional program steps as you enter them. When you enter the learn mode, the calculator is partitioned for eight program steps and four data memories. When you enter the ninth program step, the calculator automatically repartitions for 16 program steps and three data memories. This process continues to a maximum of 40 program steps and no data memories.

A Look At The Keys

Learn Key

[LRN]—Pressing this key once puts the calculator in the learn mode. This allows writing a program into program memory to be run later. Pressing [LRN] again takes the calculator out of learn mode and restores the display to its original state.

Once a calculator sequence has been determined, select the learn mode by pressing [LRN]. Then key the sequence into the program memory. The learn mode display has the following format.

00   00

Program   Instruction

Location   Code

Program locations begin at 00 and number consecutively. Each location can hold an operation or a single digit. An instruction code (or key code) is a two-digit number assigned to each operation according to its location on the keyboard. Key codes are discussed later. The calculator indicates 00 as the key code when a program is being keyed in because the calculator steps to the next available location as each instruction is keyed in.

Keeping track of the location in the program memory is the function of the program counter. In the learn mode, this counter moves step by step through the program memory, displaying the next location to be used. Entering the last step resets the program counter to step 00, takes the calculator out of learn mode, and restores the display to its original state.

Run/Stop and Reset Keys

R/S—this key reverses the status of processing. Pressing R/S starts program processing at the current position of the program counter. Pressing R/S while a program is running stops the program. However, the exact position of the program counter when the program is stopped cannot be predetermined. Entering R/S as a program step (while in the learn mode) causes program processing to stop at that point when the program is run.

2nd RST—this key resets the program counter to step 00, the beginning of the program. When used as a program step, the 2nd RST instruction does not halt program execution.

Clear Program Key

2nd CP—pressing this key while in the learn mode removes the program from program memory and resets the partitioning for five user data memories. The 2nd CP key works in the same manner outside of the learn mode. (Be careful not to accidentally press it or you will lose your program.)

Single Step and Backstep Keys

Programs may be changed in several ways. A keystroke input at any point in an existing program while in the learn mode writes over the instruction previously stored in that location. As you are editing a program and discover an unwanted instruction, press the correct instruction and it will replace the one that was displayed.

SST and BST—these keys are used in editing a program. While in the learn mode, use these keys to search through the program in order to examine or change it. The SST key moves forward one program step. The BST key moves back one step. The display shows the program step and the instruction that is in that step. The SST key can also be used to execute a program, one step at a time, with the result of each step displayed.

A Look At The Keys

Key Codes

All of the keys which can be used in programming are given numbers (key codes) which designate their location on the keyboard. They are numbered as shown in the following illustration. The first digit of the key code is the number of the row, numbered 1 through 9. The second digit is the number of the column, number 1, 2, 3, 4, and 5. The second function keys are number 6, 7, 8, 9, and 0. Thus, [ON/C] is 15, [2nd] **lnx** is 59, and [÷] is 55.

The number keys, however, all have a first digit of 0 and a second digit which is equal to the digit. Thus, 1 is 01, 2 is 02, 9 is 09, and 0 is 00. The [2nd] key does not have its own code. Instead, it changes the code of the following key. Thus, [2nd] x^2 is listed as 58 rather than 11 followed by 53.

The keys that cannot be used in programming do not have a code. These include the statistics keys and some of the programming keys such as [SST].

BA-55 Keyboard Showing Key Code and Function Name

	17 **Due**	* **Mode**		
** [2nd]	12 [CPT]	13 [R/S]	* [OFF]	15 [ON/C]
26 P/I	27 Acc	28 Bal	* NPV	* IRR
21 [N]	22 [%i]	23 [PMT]	24 [PV]	25 [FV]
* CP	37 RST			
* [LRN]	* [SST]	* [BST]	34 [APR▸]	35 [◂EFF]
* $\Sigma-$	* Corr	* Intcp	* Slope	* Fcst y
* [$\Sigma+$]	* [$\bar{x}$]	* [$\bar{y}$]	* [σn]	* [σn-1]
* Frq	57 Δ%	58 x^2	59 lnx	50 e^x
51 [$x{:}y$]	52 [%]	53 [$\sqrt{x}$]	54 [$1/x$]	55 [$\div$]
66 CLmem	67 CLmode	68 Fix	69 K	60 y^x
61 [STO]	07 [7]	08 [8]	09 [9]	65 [X]
71 [RCL]	04 [4]	05 [5]	06 [6]	75 [−]
81 [SUM]	01 [1]	02 [2]	03 [3]	85 [+]
	97 Adv	* List	99 Print	90 Trace
91 [EXC]	00 [0]	93 [.]	94 [+/−]	95 [=]

*No key code. These keys cannot be put in programs.
**This key is merged with the following keystroke.

Key Codes in Numeric Order

00—[0]	13—[R/S]	34—[APR▸]	59—lnx	85—[+]
01—[1]	15—[ON/C]	35—[◂EFF]	60—y^x	90—**Trace**
02—[2]	17—**Due**	37—**RST**	61—[STO]	91—[EXC]
03—[3]	21—[N]	50—e^x	65—[X]	93—[.]
04—[4]	22—[%i]	51—[$x{:}y$]	66—**CLmem**	94—[+/−]
05—[5]	23—[PMT]	52—[%]	67—**CLmode**	95—[=]
06—[6]	24—[PV]	53—[$\sqrt{x}$]	68—**Fix**	97—**Adv**
07—[7]	25—[FV]	54—[$1/x$]	69—K	99—**Print**
08—[8]	26—**P/I**	55—[$\div$]	71—[RCL]	
09—[9]	27—**Acc**	57— %	75—[−]	
12—[CPT]	28—**Bal**	58—x^2	81—[SUM]	

Programming Examples

Suppose you have received a sale notice from a department store indicating that all the items listed in their current catalog will be marked down 15% for one day only. There are several items that you are interested in buying, so you use your calculator to find the new price: Price ⊟ 15 [%][=]. To check the sale price of 25 different items, you have to press this key sequence 25 times. However, calculations that have to be done repeatedly are easy using the programming feature of the *Professional Business Analyst*. The program has to be entered only once. Then enter the price of each item, start the program, and the calculator executes the keystrokes in the program.

First, be sure that you are in the finance mode. Press [2nd] **Mode** until the "FIN" indicator appears in the display. Press the [LRN] key to enter the learn mode. Press [2nd] CP to clear any previous program and reset to step 00. The display changes to a unique format that indicates that the calculator is ready to learn and remember the keystrokes.

00   00

The left two digits show the program step number (from 00 to 40) and the right two show the key codes.

After entering the learn mode, press the keys needed to solve the problem. Leave the learn mode by pressing [LRN] again.

Example: Find the reduced prices on items discounted 15%. While working with money, fix the decimal at two places.

Procedure	Press	Display
1. Clear calculator and program; select two decimal places.	[ON/c] [2nd] CP [2nd] Fix 2	0.00
2. Press [2nd] **Mode** until the "FIN" indicator is displayed.	[2nd] **Mode**	0.00
3. Enter Learn Mode.	[LRN]	00 00
4. Enter [R/S] to stop program.	[R/S]	01 00
5. Calculate discount price.	[−] 15 [%][=]	06 00
6. Loop back to step 00.	[2nd] RST	07 00
7. Leave learn mode.	[LRN]	0.00

To try the program, find the discount price for $14.95, $7.50, and $24.75.

Procedure	Press	Display
1. Clear display and pending operations.	[ON/c] [ON/c]	0.00
2. Reset for first price and start program.	[2nd] RST [R/S]	0.00
3. Enter first price and run program.	14.95 [R/S]	12.71
4. Enter second price and run program.	7.5 [R/S]	6.38
5. Enter third price and run program.	24.75 [R/S]	21.04

Print Keys

The print keys located on the bottom row of the calculator are designed to function with the optional PC-200 printer. Pressing these keys without the optional printer attached may momentarily slow down calculator functions.

[2nd] **Adv**—the Advance Key causes the printer to advance the paper three lines without printing any characters. The advance key can be included in a program for separation of outputs.

[2nd] **List**—the List Key causes the contents of program memory, beginning at step 00, to be printed in sequence. The information printed includes the program step number and the key code. After printing the contents of program memory, the program counter is automatically reset to step 00. If the list function is pressed in the learn mode, the calculator leaves the learn mode and begins listing the contents of program memory. Pressing [2nd] **List** in the statistics or cash flow modes or when no program steps are allocated produces an error message.

[2nd] **Print**—the Print Key causes the display contents to be printed. The print function may be included in a program.

[2nd] **Trace**—the Trace Key causes all calculations, entries and results to be printed as they occur with the following exceptions: [STO], [RCL], [SUM], [EXC], [2nd] **Frq**, [2nd] **Fix**, live numerical entries [0] through [9], [+/−], and [·]. Pressing [2nd] **Trace** twice removes the trace mode and stops printing.

Connecting the Printer and Calculator

To connect the PC-200 and calculator, plug the connector cable into the printer port on the calculator as shown in the figure below. The printer can be connected to the calculator while the calculator is turned on.

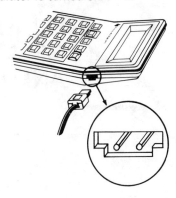

2 FUNDAMENTALS OF ANNUITIES AND CASH FLOWS

FUNDAMENTALS
OF ANNUITIES
AND CASH FLOWS
2

This chapter explains the fundamental concepts which underlie the annuities and cash flows applications of this manual. The concepts themselves are explained here while the application chapters supply examples which illustrate the techniques necessary for problem solution.

An annuity is a series of consecutive equal cash flows occurring for N equal time periods with interest calculated at the end of each cash flow period. The cash flows are usually called payments, even though they might actually represent an outflow (payment) or an inflow (receipt). The key concepts to remember in annuities are that all payments must be equal (excluding PV and FV), they must occur every time period (no missing payments), and all payments must be of the same nature (either receipts or payments).

When the payments occur at the end of each period, the annuity is called an "Ordinary Annuity" or an "Annuity in Arrears." An annuity with payments occurring at the beginning of each time period is called an "Annuity Due" or an "Advance Payment Annuity."

An annuity having payments compounded forward (negative payment value) to accumulate a future sum is often called a "Future Value Annuity" or "Compound Sum of an Annuity." When the payments are discounted back (positive payment value) to a present value, the annuity is often called a "Present Value Annuity."

Annuities

The annuities discussed in this chapter assume the number of compounding periods equals the number of payment periods per year. As a result, the annual interest rate (%I) is divided by the number of payment periods per year to determine %i. Thus, the %i annuity value is both the interest rate per payment period and the interest rate per compounding period.

Both ordinary annuities and annuities due assume an equal number of payment and compounding periods per year with interest compounded at the end of each payment period. As a result, the only difference between an annuity due and an ordinary annuity is the number of compounding periods. Since the first annuity due payment occurs at the beginning of period one while the first ordinary annuity payment occurs at the end of period one, the compounding effects produce different PV and FV values.

An annuity due with payments compounded forward (negative payment value) to accumulate a future sum is a Future Value Annuity Due. When the beginning-of-period payments are discounted back (positive payment value) to a present value, the annuity is a Present Value Annuity Due. Annuity due problems are solved the same as ordinary annuities, except that the (2nd) **Due** key is pressed before the unknown value key.

So far in explaining annuities, either PV or FV as input or unknown value has been used, but not both at the same time. This approach facilitates the explanation of ordinary annuities in a traditional fashion. The compound interest and annuity keys, however, allow both PV and FV as inputs, or either value as an unknown with the other as an input. This feature gives the calculator flexibility for solving advanced financial and real estate problems. A number of time value of money applications, such as bonds, capital budgeting, leasing, and balloon mortgages, require combining a present value annuity and compound interest. These annuities are called present value annuities with an ending balloon payment. The term present value annuities is used not because they have only a present value (PV), but because the future value (FV) and payment (PMT) are of the same nature (both inflows or outflows) and are discounted back to equal the present value. The annuity involved may be either an ordinary annuity or an annuity due.

There are two assumptions to remember when solving these annuities: the PV value *always* occurs at the *beginning* of the *first payment period* and the FV value *always* occurs at the *end* of the *last payment period*. Otherwise, the calculator operates as before, with discounting indicated by entering a positive PMT value and compounding indicated by entering a negative value.

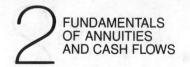

End of Period Regular Payments (Ordinary Annuity) With Ending Balloon

The cash flow pattern can be illustrated by drawing the ordinary annuity and the compound interest diagrams and then combining them as shown below.

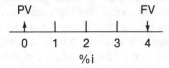

Compound Interest Time-line Diagram

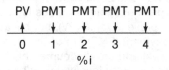

Present Value Ordinary Annuity Time-line Diagram

Combining a present value ordinary annuity with compound interest where both the payments and future value are either cash inflows or cash outflows results in the following time-line diagram.

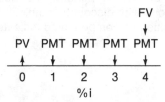

**Basic Time-line Diagram for Combining a
Present Value Ordinary Annuity with Compound Interest**

This combined time-line diagram represents the cash flow pattern for a mortgage with a final extra payment usually called a balloon. The FV occurs at the same point in time as the last regular payment and the combined PV occurs at the beginning of the first payment period (time 0). Also, the direction of the cash flows for the regular payments and the future value are the same. This is important because the calculator assumes this cash flow pattern when a positive PMT, PV, and FV are entered or solved for in a problem.

Solving for the present value or any other value in a combined annuity and compound interest problem is a simple task with the compound interest and annuity keys once you have identified the inputs for the problem. The definition of N is now the total number of equal regular payments. You indicate discounting for an annuity by entering the payment as a positive value (no sign needs to be entered with the value). For ordinary annuities, the solution sequence requires that CPT be pressed before pressing the unknown value key. See the application entitled "Mortgages with Balloon Payments or Early Payoff" in Chapter 5 for an example of ordinary annuity payments with ending balloon payment.

For an example of an ordinary annuity where payments are compounded forward, see the application entitled "Sinking Fund, Solving for Payment Amount" in Chapter 4.

2 FUNDAMENTALS
OF ANNUITIES
AND CASH FLOWS

Beginning of Period Payments (Annuity Due) With Ending Balloon

The cash flow pattern can be illustrated by drawing the annuity due and the compound interest diagrams and then combining them as shown below.

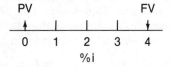

Compound interest time-line diagram

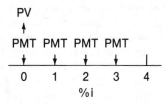

Present value annuity due time-line diagram

Combining a present value annuity due with compound interest results in the following cash flow pattern if both the payments and future value are either cash inflows or cash outflows.

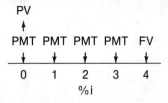

**Basic time-line diagram for combining a
present value annuity due with compound interest**

This combined time-line diagram represents the cash flow pattern for a lease with a final extra payment usually called a residual value. The FV occurs at the end of the last payment period and one period after the last regular payment. The combined PV occurs at the beginning of the first payment period (time 0). Also, the direction of the cash flows for the regular payments and the future value is the same. This is important since the compound interest and annuity keys assume this cash flow pattern when a positive PMT, PV, and FV are entered or solved for in a problem.

Solving for annuities due with ending balloon is identical to solving for ordinary annuities except that the solution sequence requires that [2nd] **Due** be pressed before pressing the unknown value key. When [2nd] **Due** is pressed, the calculator automatically assumes that payments occur at the beginning of each period when solving for an unknown annuity value. See the application entitled "Determining Payment Amount" in Chapter 7 for an example of an annuity due with balloon payment.

For an example of an annuity due with payments compounded forward, see the application entitled "Applications with a Series of Equal Deposits and a Beginning Balance, Finding Future Value" in Chapter 9.

FUNDAMENTALS
OF ANNUITIES
AND CASH FLOWS

In annuities, all payments are equal, periodic, and of the same nature (inflow or outflow). A more general case, however, is a series of unequal cash flows, each either an inflow or an outflow. These unequal cash flows are usually called *Variable Cash Flows* or *Uneven Cash Flows*. Furthermore, you can have a series of cash flows that remain constant for a number of payment periods and then change to a different amount for a number of periods. Cash flows having such a pattern are often called *Grouped Cash Flows*.

You can compute the Net Present Value or the Internal Rate of Return directly on your calculator for 10 different cash flows and a time period zero cash flow, or 10 groups of cash flows from one up to 999 cash flows in each group and a time period zero cash flow. Depending on the solution key sequence, cash flows can be placed at the end or the beginning of each payment period.

End of Period Cash Flows

This section explains how to use your calculator to compute the net present value or the interest rate for a series of end-of-period uneven cash flows. The only new terms introduced are CFm and NPV. While the term PMT is used to describe the periodic, equal payment for an annuity, the term CFm is used to describe the mth cash flow for uneven cash flows. The term NPV is the difference between the cash flow at time period zero and the present value of the future cash flows if the initial cash flow is an outflow and the subsequent cash flows are inflows.

Consider this diagram with five unequal cash flows:

NPV = ?

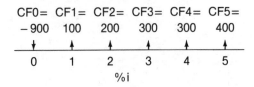

The calculator computes the present value of each cash flow and sums them together to determine the total present value.

Net Present Value = PV0 + PV1 + PV2 + PV3 + PV4 + PV5

The uneven cash flow problem can be reduced to a series of compound interest problems. But, unlike annuities, one equation to compute the present value cannot be developed since the cash flows vary. Therefore, your calculator program computes the present value one cash flow at a time and then sums them together for the total present value. This solution sequence occurs when you press [CPT] [2nd] **NPV**.

Net present value is the present value of the future cash flows discounted at the specified interest rate plus the time zero cash flows. If the time zero cash flow is an outflow and the future cash flows are inflows, then the NPV is the difference between the two values. But, if all cash flows including the zero period cash flow are either inflows or outflows, the net present value is simply the sum of all the individual discounted cash flows.

The interest rate that makes the series of cash flows discount to equal a net present value of zero is computed using a Newton-Raphson method which is suitable for a calculator or computer but impractical for manual solution. This interest rate is usually called the Internal Rate of Return. For end of period cash flows, the solution sequence is [CPT] [2nd] **IRR**. See the application entitled "Capital Budgeting, Determining Net Present Value and Rate of Return with Variable Cash Flows and Accelerated Depreciation" in Chapter 11 for an example of determining internal rate of return and net present value with end of period cash flows.

Variable And Grouped Cash Flows

Beginning of Period Cash Flows

When the [2nd] **Due** key is used for solving either NPV or IRR, the calculator automatically places the cash flows at the beginning of each payment period. This is illustrated by the cash flows shown in the following diagram.

```
        NPV = ?
      CF0 = - 900

        CF1=  CF2=  CF3=  CF4=  CF5=
        100   200   300   300   400
         ↓     ↓     ↓     ↓     ↓      |
        0     1     2     3     4      5
                    % i
```

These are the same cash flows used to illustrate the end of payment period concepts, but now each cash flow occurs at the beginning of the cash flow period. Notice that both cash flow zero (– 900) and the first payment (CF1) occur at the same point in time. You enter the time period zero cash flow in the PV register, and the remaining cash flows as before; then, when [2nd] **Due NPV** or [2nd] **Due IRR** is pressed, the calculator automatically shifts the payments to the beginning of each period. This is a convenient feature for analyzing leases with grouped or variable payments. You can also determine the difference between receiving payments at the end or beginning of each period by solving using the [CPT] key sequence and then the [2nd] **Due** key sequence without reentering the cash flows. See the application entitled "Leases with Variable Payments, Computing Interest Rate Earned" in Chapter 7 for an example of determining internal rate of return and net present value with beginning of period cash flows.

Converting Annual Interest Rates

In the United States, annual interest rates are normally defined as Annual Nominal Rates or Annual Percentage Rates (APR). The annual rate is found by multiplying the interest rate per compounding period and the number of compounding periods per year. A loan having a 1% monthly compounding rate has an annual rate of 12%.

In the previous discussion of cash flows, the number of payment periods and the number of compounding periods per year were equal. This is a valid assumption in many situations, but it is not valid in others. For example, savings and loan associations may compound interest daily while deposits are made monthly. Furthermore, in many investment situations the number of compounding periods per year may differ from investment to investment. This means the comparison of APRs is misleading. In such situations, a comparison of the annual effective rates is the true measure.

Consider an investment of $1 for 12 months with an APR of 12% compounded monthly. The value of the investment at the year's end is $1.12682503. This is summarized on the time-line diagram below.

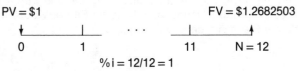

You can also ask the following question, "What annual interest rate compounded once a year yields the same future value?" Drawing a second time-line diagram illustrates this question:

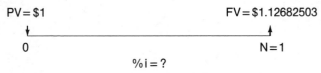

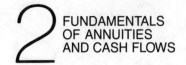
The answer to the question is the interest rate that makes $1
grow to $1.12682503 in one compounding period. Since $1 is
invested, the interest earned is $.12682503, or expressed as a
percent, 12.682503%. Hence, the annual effective interest
rate is 12.682503%. By definition, the annual effective rate is
compounded annually. This annual effective rate is
equivalent to a monthly rate of 1% compounded 12 times a
year, which is also a nominal rate (or APR) of 12%. You cannot make a meaningful comparison of APRs by ranking them
if each APR has a different number of compounding periods
per year. The annual effective rate of each should be
calculated before ranking the projects. For more information
about annual percentage rates and annual effective rates,
see the application entitled "Finding Interest Rate (Yield)
when the Buyer Pays Points" and "Applications with a
Series of Variable Deposits, Solving for Future Value" in
Chapter 5 and Appendix A.

3 PRICING

PRICING 3

The factors which influence the selling price of an item also significantly affect your purchasing power. When you are buying merchandise, the final purchase price is affected by sales taxes, discounts, and markups. On the other side of the transaction, the selling price of merchandise is determined by the amount the merchant paid (cost) and the merchant's gross profit margin (GPM) or markup. The same basic considerations are involved in sales tax and markup:

Sales Tax
Price Plus Tax = Price Before Tax (1 + Tax%)

or

Markup
Sales Price = Cost (1 + Markup%)

However, gross profit margins, markdowns, and discounts are computed as a percentage of the selling price and use the following basic formulas:

Gross Profit Margin
$$\text{Selling Price} = \frac{\text{Cost}}{(1 - \text{GPM\%})}$$

Discounts
$$\text{Selling Price} = \frac{\text{Cost}}{(1 - \text{discount\%})}$$

Markdowns
$$\text{Selling Price} = \frac{\text{Cost}}{(1 - \text{markdown\%})}$$

Sample problems involving sales tax, markups, GPM, discounts, and markdowns are illustrated in this chapter. The chapter ends with a series of examples showing the impact of inflation on gross profit margins and cash flows. By having your calculator perform the tedious arithmetical calculations, you can concentrate on making the sale and increasing the profit potential of your business. And, if you're the consumer, your calculator can give you a breakdown of your expenses.

PRICING

Determining Sales Tax and Price

You are buying a new sorting machine from a local business supply store and have agreed on a price of $4,632 plus 4% sales tax. How much will the tax and the total cost be?

Procedure	Press	Display
1. Clear calculator and select two decimal places.	[ON/c] [2nd] Fix 2	**0.00**
2. Enter purchase price.	4632 [+]	**4632.00**
3. Enter tax rate and compute sales tax.	4 [%]	**185.28**
4. Compute purchase price plus tax.	[=]	**4817.28**

The sales tax is $185.28, and the total cost is $4,817.28.

Determining Price Before Sales Tax

You and a salesman have just agreed that the final price you'll pay for a refrigerator is $550.00, including the 6% sales tax. How much are you paying for the refrigerator, and how much is paid in taxes?

Procedure	Press	Display
1. Clear calculator and select two decimal places.	[ON/c] [2nd] Fix 2	**0.00**
2. Enter tax.	6 [%] [+] 1 [=] [1/x]	**0.94**
3. Enter after-tax price, and compute before-tax price.	[×] 550 [=]	**518.87**
4. Enter after-tax price and compute tax.	[+/−] [+] 550 [=]	**31.13**

The price of the refrigerator is $518.87, and the tax is $31.13.

PRICING

Determining Cost Before Markup

The list price of a certain microwave oven is $342.56, and the store's markup is 22% of cost. How much did the microwave oven cost the store?

Procedure	Press	Display
1. Clear calculator and select two decimal places.	⟨ON/C⟩ ⟨2nd⟩ **Fix** 2	0.00
2. Enter markup and compute cost as decimal percent of price.	22 ⟨%⟩ ⟨+⟩ 1 ⟨=⟩ ⟨1/x⟩	0.82
3. Enter list price and compute cost.	⟨X⟩ 342.56 ⟨=⟩	280.79

The store's cost is $280.79 or 82% of list price.

Determining Markups and Selling Prices

A grocery store manager has purchased a load of bananas for $0.21 per pound. At what price should he sell the bananas if his standard markup is 20% of cost?

Procedure	Press	Display
1. Clear calculator and select two decimal places.	⟨ON/C⟩ ⟨2nd⟩ **Fix** 2	0.00
2. Enter cost.	.21 ⟨+⟩	0.21
3. Enter markup percent and compute markup dollars.	20 ⟨%⟩	0.04
4. Compute selling price.	⟨=⟩	0.25

The selling price should be $0.25 per pound.

Discounts

Determining the Discount

A store near your home recently advertised a lawnmower which usually sells for $239.45 at a 15% discount. What is the sale price?

Procedure	Press	Display
1. Clear calculator and select two decimal places.	ON/c 2nd **Fix 2**	**0.00**
2. Enter regular price.	239.45 −	**239.45**
3. Enter discount percent and compute dollar amount.	15 %	**35.92**
4. Compute price less discount.	=	**203.53**

The sale price of the lawnmower is $203.53.

Determining Price Before Discount

A stereo system is on sale for $323.55. The salesman explains that the sale price is a 35% savings from the regular price. What is the regular price?

Procedure	Press	Display
1. Clear calculator and select two decimal places.	ON/c 2nd **Fix 2**	**0.00**
2. Enter discount.	1 − 35	
	% = 1/x	**1.54**
3. Enter sale price and compute regular price.	× 323.55 =	**497.77**

The price was $497.77 before discount.

Calculating the Selling Price Necessary to Earn a Specified GPM

You need to determine the retail price for an item that cost your store $22.50. If you require a 35% gross profit margin on sales, what should the retail price be?

Procedure	Press	Display
1. Clear calculator and select two decimal places.	[ON/c][2nd] **Fix** 2	**0.00**
2. Enter percentage of gross profit margin.	1 [−] 35 [%][=][1/x]	**1.54**
3. Enter cost and calculate selling price.	[X] 22.50 [=]	**34.62**

The retail price should be $34.62.

Calculating the Dealer's Cost, Based on GPM

A new compact car on a showroom floor has a base sticker price of $5,100. You read in a consumer magazine that compacts are generally priced to provide the dealer about a 17% margin on the selling price. If this report is correct, how much did the car cost the dealer?

Procedure	Press	Display
1. Clear calculator and select two decimal places.	[ON/c][2nd] **Fix** 2	**0.00**
2. Enter selling price.	5100 [−]	**5100.00**
3. Enter margin as a percentage.	17 [%]	**867.00**
4. Calculate cost.	[=]	**4233.00**

Assuming a 17% margin, the cost was $4,233.

PRICING

Calculating Margin (GPM)

You are making macrame bags and your total material,
labor, and incidental costs per bag are $13.75. A local store
pays you $17.47 for each bag you make. What is your gross
profit margin (GPM) on selling price?

Procedure	Press	Display
1. Clear calculator and select two decimal places.	[ON/c][2nd] Fix 2	**0.00**
2. Enter cost.	13.75 [2nd] Δ%	**13.75**
3. Enter selling price.	17.47	**17.47**
4. Calculate GPM.	[=][+/−]	**21.29**

Your GPM is 21.29%.

The examples in this section show you inflation's impact on cash flows and profits when the replacement cost is considered. In general, taxes and income statements are computed using the historical cost. But you pay the replacement cost when replacing products you sell.

Determining Cash Available After Replacing a Product

Assume that on June 1, 1982, you paid $100 for a product which you held for resale. On January 1, 1983, you sell the product for $125. With an annual inflation rate of 18% compounded monthly applied to the wholesale price of this product, how much will you pay to replace the product? If your tax rate is 40%, how much cash will you have after replacing the product?

If the memory indicator does not show at least two data memories available, press [2nd] **CP** before keying in the example.

Effects Of Inflation

3 PRICING

Procedure	Press	Display
1. Clear calculator and mode registers; select two decimal places.	ON/C 2nd **CLmode** 2nd **Fix 2**	0.00
2. Press 2nd Mode until the "FIN" indicator is displayed.	2nd **Mode**	0.00
3. Enter number of months product was held.	7 N	7.00
4. Enter periodic inflation rate.	18 ÷ 12 = %i	1.50
5. Enter original cost of product.	100 PV	100.00
6. Compute and store replacement cost.	CPT FV STO 1	110.98
7. Enter selling price and sub-tract original cost to calculate amount of tax-able income and store.	125 − 100 = STO 2	25.00
8. Multiply by tax rate to calculate income tax and add to replacement cost stored in memory.	× 40 % = SUM 1	10.00
9. Enter selling price. Calculate cash available after replacing product and paying taxes.	125 − RCL 1 =	4.02
10. Calculate cash available without inflation (subtract tax from difference in sell-ing price and original cost).	RCL 2 − 40 % =	15.00

After replacing the product, you have $4.02 available cash, compared to $15 without inflation.

Determining Selling Price to Achieve a Specified Gross Margin (GPM)

You have found that a product which originally cost you $100 can now be sold for $125, resulting in a gross margin of 20% based on historical cost. The replacement cost with inflation is $110.98. Find the sales price necessary to maintain a 20% gross margin when the cost of goods sold is based on the replacement cost.

	Procedure	Press	Display
1.	Clear calculator and select two decimal places.	[ON/c] [2nd] Fix 2	**0.00**
2.	Enter selling price and original cost, and compute gross profit margin.	100 [2nd] Δ% 125 [=] [+/-]	**20.00**
3.	Subtract gross profit margin decimal value from one.	[%] [-] 1 [=] [+/-]	**0.80**
4.	Enter replacement cost.	[÷] 110.98	**110.98**
5.	Compute sales price using replacement cost.	[=] [1/x]	**138.73**

For a gross margin of 20% and a replacement cost of $110.98, you need to sell the product for $138.73.

Determining Sales Price to Achieve a Specified After-Tax Cash Flow

If a product which was originally purchased for $100 has a replacement cost of $110.98 and the tax rate is 40%, find the sales price necessary to have a $15 cash flow after paying taxes and replacing the product (the amount of cash that would be available without inflation).

If the memory indicator does not show at least two data memories available, press [2nd] **CP** before entering the solution.

Procedure	Press	Display
1. Clear calculator and select two decimal places.	[ON/C] [2nd] **Fix** 2	**0.00**
2. Press [2nd] **Mode** until the "FIN" indicator is displayed.	[2nd] **Mode**	**0.00**
3. Enter required after-tax cash flow.	15	**15**
4. Add replacement cost and store result.	[+] 110.98 [=] [STO] 1	**125.98**
5. Enter original cost and multiply by tax rate; subtract from memory.	100 [×] 40 [%] [=] [+/-] [SUM] 1	**−40.00**
6. Subtract tax rate from 100 and convert to decimal to calculate after-tax rate; store results.	100 [−] 40 [=] [%] [STO] 2	**0.60**
7. Divide value in memory one by value in memory two to calculate sale price.	[RCL] 1 [÷] [RCL] 2 [=]	**143.30**

You will need to sell the product for $143.30 if you want an after-tax cash flow of $15.

4 ACCOUNTING

ACCOUNTING 4

This chapter has a number of applications that are particularly useful to both practitioners and students of accounting. Four methods of depreciation are discussed. They are straight-line, sum-of-the-years'-digits, declining balance, and accelerated cost recovery system. The breakeven point and net income are estimated with cost-volume-profit analysis. Amortization of leases, bonds, and notes receivable is the next topic discussed. The chapter concludes with a discussion of ordinary sinking funds and sinking funds with changing deposits and interest rates.

Depreciation

Straight-Line

The ABC Company purchases a machine on April 1 for
$5,000 that has a $750 salvage value with a five year life.
Compute the depreciation expense for each year using the
straight-line method.*

If the memory indicator does not show at least two data
memories available, press 2nd CP before entering the
solution.

Procedure	Press	Display
1. Clear calculator and select two decimal places.	ON/c 2nd Fix 2	0.00
2. Press 2nd Mode until the "FIN" indicator is displayed.	2nd Mode	0.00
3. Calculate depreciable value (cost − salvage value).	5000 − 750 =	4250.00
4. Divide by life of asset to calculate annual depreciation and store.	÷ 5 = STO 1	850.00
5. Calculate and store depreciation for year one (April 1 to Dec. 31 = nine months or 9/12 years).	× 9 ÷ 12 = STO 2	637.50
6. Calculate depreciation for year six (Jan. 1 to March 31 = three months) and add to memory.	RCL 1 × 3 ÷ 12 = SUM 2	212.50
7. Calculate depreciation for years two, three, four, and five (a total of four years) and add to memory.	RCL 1 × 4 = SUM 2	3400.00
8. Recall total accumulated depreciation. (This value should equal the depreciable value.)	RCL 2	4250.00

*See Appendix A for the formula.

Without partial year depreciation, the annual depreciation is $850 per year for five years. With partial year depreciation, however, the depreciation is $637.50 for year one, $850 for year's two through five, and $212.50 for year six.

Sum-of-the-Years'-Digits

The ABC Company purchases a machine on April 1 for $5,000 that has a $750 salvage value with a five-year life. Compute the depreciation expense for each year using the SYD method.*

If the memory indicator does not show at least four data memories available, press [2nd] **CP** before entering the solution.

Procedure	Press	Display
1. Clear calculator and select two decimal places.	[ON/c] [2nd] Fix 2	**0.00**
2. Press [2nd] **Mode** until the "FIN" indicator is displayed.	[2nd] **Mode**	**0.00**
3. Enter and store life in years.	5 [STO] 1	**5.00**
4. Calculate sum of years in months and store.	[+] 1 [×] [RCL] 1 [×] 6 [=] [STO] 2	**180.00**
5. Calculate depreciable value (cost − salvage value).	5000 [−] 750 [=]	**4250.00**
6. Divide depreciable value by sum of years in months and store. Multiply by 12 to calculate yearly value and store.	[÷] [RCL] 2 [=] [STO] 2 [×] 12 [=] [STO] 3	**283.33**
7. Enter and store months of depreciation taken in fiscal year one.	9 [STO] 4	**9.00**
		(continued)

*See Appendix A for the formulas.

(continued)

Procedure	Press	Display
8. Calculate depreciation for fiscal year one.	⊠ RCL 1 ⊠ RCL 2 =	1062.50
9. Calculate depreciation for fiscal year two.	12 ⊠ RCL 1 – RCL 4 ⊠ RCL 2 =	1204.17
10. Calculate depreciation for remaining fiscal years.		
a. Fiscal year three.	– RCL 3 =	920.83
b. Fiscal year four.	– RCL 3 =	637.50
c. Fiscal year five.	– RCL 3 =	354.17
d. Fiscal year six.	– RCL 3 =	70.83

The depreciation expense is $1,062.50 for fiscal year one, $1,204.17 for year two, $920.83 for year three, $637.50 for year four, $354.17 for year five, and $70.83 for year six.

Note that this keystroke sequence assumes the asset life is in whole years with partial years of depreciation allocated by whole months. If no partial year depreciation is taken, enter twelve months in step seven.

Declining Balance

The ABC Company purchases a machine on April 1 for $5,000 that has a $750 salvage value with a five-year life. Compute the depreciation expense for each year using the declining balance method*. For this example, use a 200% factor. Note also that the depreciation stops when the depreciable value equals the salvage value, while the SYD and SL methods continue until the end of the asset life.

If the memory indicator does not show at least one data memory available, press 2nd CP before keying in the example.

*See Appendix A for the formula.

Procedure	Press	Display
1. Clear calculator and select two decimal places.	[ON/c] [2nd] **Fix** 2	**0.00**
2. Press [2nd] **Mode** until the "FIN" indicator is displayed.	[2nd] **Mode**	**0.00**
3. Divide declining-balance factor by life in years and store.	200 [÷] 5 [=] [STO] 1	**40.00**
4. Calculate first partial-year depreciation.		
a. Multiply by cost to calculate depreciation for first calendar year.	[%] [X] 5000 [=]	**2000.00**
b. Enter month and calculate partial-year depreciation.	[X] 9 [÷] 12 [=]	**1500.00**
5. Calculate net book value at start of second year.	[+/−] [+] 5000 [=]	**3500.00**
6. Calculate depreciation expense for second year.	[−] [RCL] 1 [%]	**1400.00**
7. Calculate net book value at end of second year.	[=]	**2100.00**
8. Calculate depreciation expense for third year.	[−] [RCL] 1 [%]	**840.00**
9. Calculate net book value at end of third year.	[=]	**1260.00**
10. Calculate depreciation expense for fourth year.	[−] [RCL] 1 [%]	**504.00**
11. Calculate net book value at end of fourth year.	[=]	**756.00**
12. Calculate depreciation expense for fifth year.	[−] 750 [=]	**6.00**

Depreciation

Depreciation

The depreciation stops in year five with a depreciation expense of $6.00 because the net book value in year six is less than the $750 salvage value after depreciation is computed using the regular procedure.

Note: For whole year depreciation, omit step 4b.

Accelerated Cost Recovery System

The Economic Recovery Tax Act of 1981 provides a depreciation procedure called the accelerated cost recovery system (ACRS). This method uses declining-balance depreciation during the asset's early life with a switch to straight-line depreciation during the latter years. The ACRS method assumes all assets are depreciated one-half year during the year of acquisition and have a zero salvage value. A set of tables is provided to calculate the ACRS depreciation. The tables vary depending on the date of purchase. One of these tables are reproduced below.

Assets purchased during 1981-1984

Applicable percentage per year

Life/years	1	2	3	4	5	6	7	8	9	10
3 years	25	38	37							
5 years	15	22	21	21	21					
10 years	8	14	12	10	10	10	9	9	9	9

The depreciation expense for each year is equal to the cost multiplied by the applicable percentage from the table.

The ABC Company purchases a machine for $5,000 in 1982. It qualified for five-year ACRS depreciation. Compute the depreciation expense for the annual tax return.

If the memory indicator does not show at least one data memory available, press [2nd] CP before keying in the example.

Procedure	Press	Display
1. Clear calculator and fix decimal to two places.	[ON/C][2nd] Fix 2	**0.00**
2. Press [2nd] **Mode** until the "FIN" indicator is displayed.	[2nd] **Mode**	**0.00**
3. Store asset cost.	5000 [STO] 1	**5000.00**
4. Enter percentage for year one and calculate depreciation.	[X] 15 [%][=]	**750.00**
5. Enter percentage for year two and calculate depreciation.	[RCL] 1 [X] 22 [%][=]	**1100.00**
6. Enter percentage for years three, four, and five; calculate depreciation.	[RCL] 1 [X] 21 [%][=]	**1050.00**

The depreciation expenses for years one through five are $750, $1,100, $1,050, $1,050, and $1,050.

Cost-Volume-
Profit Analysis

A canoe company sells its paddles for $20 each. The unit variable cost is $15, and fixed costs are $3,000. The company's tax rate is 40%. Assuming that all paddles produced are sold and all costs remain the same, what is the breakeven point? What sales volume (in dollars and units) must be reached to earn $2,500 after taxes? What after-tax income is produced by $34,000 in sales?

If the memory indicator does not show at least two data memories available, press 2nd CP before entering the solution.

Procedure	Press	Display
1. Clear calculator; select two decimal places.	ON/c 2nd **Fix** 2	**0.00**
2. Press 2nd **Mode** until the "FIN" indicator is displayed.	2nd **Mode**	**0.00**
3. Divide unit cost by selling price.	15 ÷ 20 =	**0.75**
4. Subtract displayed number from one to calculate contribution margin as a decimal; store result.	+/− + 1 = STO 1	**0.25**
5. Enter fixed cost and store.	3000 STO 2	**3000.00**
6. Calculate breakeven point in dollars.	÷ RCL 1 =	**12000.00**
7. Divide by selling price to calculate breakeven point in units.	÷ 20 =	**600.00**

(continued)

(continued)

Procedure	Press	Display
8. Solve for sales to earn specified after-tax income.		
a. Subtract tax rate from one.	1 ⊟ 40 ⟮%⟯ ⟮=⟯	**0.60**
b. Find reciprocal of displayed number and multiply by specified income to calculate income *before* taxes.	⟮1/x⟯⟮×⟯ 2500 ⟮=⟯	**4166.67**
c. Add fixed costs and divide by contribution margin to determine dollar sales.	⟮+⟯⟮RCL⟯ 2 ⟮÷⟯⟮RCL⟯ 1 ⟮=⟯	**28666.67**
d. Divide by sales price to find sales volume in units.	⟮÷⟯ 20 ⟮=⟯	**1433.33**
9. Solve for after-tax income earned.		
a. Enter sales and multiply by contribution margin.	34000 ⟮×⟯⟮RCL⟯ 1 ⟮=⟯	**8500.00**
b. Subtract fixed costs to determine income before taxes.	⟮−⟯⟮RCL⟯ 2 ⟮=⟯	**5500.00**
c. Enter tax rate to compute after-tax income.	⟮−⟯ 40 ⟮%⟯⟮=⟯	**3300.00**

The breakeven point is $12,000 or 600 units. To earn $2,500 after taxes, 1,433.33 units must be sold at $20 each giving total sales of $28,666.67. For sales of $34,000, the after-tax income is $3,300.

Bond Premium or Discount (Effective Interest Method)

This method assumes that bond interest expense is computed using the effective interest rate times the bond book value rather than the nominal rate times the par value. The cash paid out, however, is computed using the nominal interest rate times the par value. The difference between the interest expense and the cash payment is the bond premium or discount. This amount is added to the bond book value if it is a discount, and is subtracted from the bond book value if it is a premium. The adjusted book value is used for the interest expense computation for the next period.

The LB Tennis Ranch has issued $100,000 worth of bonds for $93,204.84. The bonds mature in ten years and have a nominal rate of 7% with a semi-annual coupon. The effective interest rate or yield is 8%. Calculate the bond discount, interest, and balance after interest for coupon periods 1 and 10.

Procedure	Press	Display
1. Clear calculator and mode registers; select two decimal places.	ON/c 2nd **CLmode** 2nd **Fix 2**	**0.00**
2. Press 2nd **Mode** until the "FIN" indicator is displayed.	2nd **Mode**	**0.00**
3. Calculate and enter periodic yield.	8 ÷ 2 = %i	**4.00**
4. Calculate and enter coupon payment.	7 % × 100000 ÷ 2 = PMT	**3500.00**
5. Enter bond cost.	93204.84 PV	**93204.84**
6. Enter coupon period number and calculate bond discount (negative answer) or premium (positive value).	1 CPT 2nd P/I	**−228.19**
7. Compute bond interest expense.	x:y	**3728.19**
8. Compute net book value at end of period.	1 CPT 2nd Bal	**93433.03**

Repeat steps 6-8 for each coupon period.

Period 10		
Discount/Premium	10 CPT 2nd P/I	**−324.79**
Interest	x:y	**3824.79**
Net book value	10 CPT 2nd Bal	**95944.56**

Note: You can use the mortgage amortization schedule program shown in this chapter to solve for the schedule and get a printout if you have a printer.

Reference: Kieso and Weygandt, *Intermediate Accounting*.

Leasehold

Leasehold amortization requires computing the present value of lease payments using an appropriate discount rate. This lease obligation is amortized over the life of the lease with the annual lease payment being separated into two components—interest on the unpaid obligation and reduction of the lease obligation. The schedules can differ depending on the timing of the payments. The solution for leases with payments made at the beginning of the period is shown below.

A firm has leased some equipment for four years and has agreed to pay the annual $5,000 lease payments at the beginning of each year. They have also guaranteed the residual value of $7,000 at the end of the lease term. Assuming an annual implicit interest rate of 6%, determine the present value of the lease and prepare a leasehold amortization schedule.

Procedure	Press	Display
1. Clear calculator and mode registers; select two decimal places.	[ON/c] [2nd] **CLmode** [2nd] **Fix 2**	0.00
2. Press [2nd] **Mode** until the "FIN" indicator is displayed.	[2nd] **Mode**	0.00
3. Enter total number of regular lease payments.	4 [N]	4.00
4. Enter periodic interest rate.	6 [%i]	6.00
5. Enter lease payment.	5000 [PMT]	5000.00
6. Enter residual value.	7000 [FV]	7000.00
7. Determine present value of lease.	[2nd] **Due** [PV]	23909.72
8. Enter payment number and compute reduction in lease balance.	1 [2nd] **Due** [2nd] **P/I**	5000.00
9. Compute interest.	[x:y]	0.00

(continued)

(continued)

Procedure	Press	Display
10. Enter payment number and compute balance after payment.	1 [2nd] **Due** [2nd] **Bal**	18909.72
11. Repeat steps 8-10 for each payment.		
a. Second payment.		
Principal.	2 [2nd] **Due** [2nd] **P/I**	3865.42
Interest.	[x:y]	1134.58
Balance.	2 [2nd] **Due** [2nd] **Bal**	15044.30
b. Third payment.		
Principal.	3 [2nd] **Due** [2nd] **P/I**	4097.34
Interest.	[x:y]	902.66
Balance.	3 [2nd] **Due** [2nd] **Bal**	10946.96
c. Fourth payment.		
Principal.	4 [2nd] **Due** [2nd] **P/I**	4343.18
Interest.	[x:y]	656.82
Balance.	4 [2nd] **Due** [2nd] **Bal**	6603.77
12. Compute residual value at end of fourth year.	[PV] 1 [N] 0 [PMT] [CPT] [FV]	7000.00

The present value of the lease is $23,909.72. Because you are amortizing beginning of period payments, the balance shown after the fourth payment is the balance at the beginning of the year. You must compound the beginning balance forward one period to determine the residual value at the *end* of the period.

ACCOUNTING

Companies occasionally establish sinking funds to accumulate a given amount for bond refunding, equipment purchase, or other commitment. Sinking funds normally assume that deposits are made at the end of each payment period.

Solving for Payment Amount

Your company wants to have $50,000 in a sinking fund at the end of five years. An initial deposit of $10,000 will be made along with semi-annual payments at the end of each period into an account paying 7% annual rate compounded semi-annually. Find the amount of the semi-annual deposit.

Procedure	Press	Display
1. Clear calculator and mode registers; select two decimal places.	ON/c 2nd **CLmode** 2nd **Fix** 2	0.00
2. Press 2nd **Mode** until the "FIN" indicator is displayed.	2nd **Mode**	0.00
3. Enter years; calculate and enter number of equal deposits.	5 ✕ 2 ═ N	10.00
4. Enter annual interest and calculate periodic interest rate.	7 ÷ 2 ═ %i	3.50
5. Enter initial deposit (if no initial deposit or balance enter zero).	10000 PV	10000.00
6. Enter future value of sinking fund.	50000 FV	50000.00
7. Compute payment.	CPT PMT	– 3059.65

Semi-annual deposits of $3,059.65 along with the initial deposit of $10,000 will compound to $50,000 after five years.

Computing a Schedule of Interest Earned

Accountants often need to determine the amount of interest earned on a sinking fund for verifying interest earned or for making journal entries. This example shows the procedure for determining the interest earned during a single payment period or over a number of payment periods.

Your company is depositing $3,000 at the end of each quarter in a sinking fund. On January 1, 1981, an initial deposit of $8,000 was made. Three months later, the first regular deposit of $3,000 was made. The annual interest rate of 7% is compounded quarterly. What is the amount of interest earned during the first and second quarters as well as the interest earned during the first and second years? What is the balance after two years?

ACCOUNTING

	Procedure	Press	Display
1.	Clear calculator and mode registers; select two decimal places.	[ON/c] [2nd] **CLmode** [2nd] **Fix 2**	**0.00**
2.	Press [2nd] **Mode** until the "FIN" indicator is displayed.	[2nd] **Mode**	**0.00**
3.	Calculate and enter periodic interest rate.	7 [÷] 4 [=] [%i]	**1.75**
4.	Enter amount of initial deposit.	8000 [PV]	**8000.00**
5.	Enter amount of regular deposit as a negative number.	3000 [+/−] [PMT]	**−3000.00**

Compute Interest Earned During a Period.

6.	Enter deposit number and compute interest earned during first quarter.	1 [CPT] [2nd] P/I [x:y]	**140.00**
7.	Compute interest earned during the second quarter.	2 [CPT] [2nd] P/I [x:y]	**194.95**

Compute Interest Earned Over a Period of Time.

8.	Enter number of deposits in first year and compute interest earned and store.	4 [CPT] [2nd] Acc [STO] 1	**893.56**
9.	Enter total number of deposits over two years and subtract value from step eight to compute interest earned in year two.	8 [CPT] [2nd] Acc [−] [RCL] 1 [=]	**1820.08**
10.	Compute balance after eight deposits.	8 [CPT] [2nd] Bal	**34713.65**

The fund earned $140.00 during the first quarter and $194.95 during the second quarter. The interest earned in the first year is $893.56 and $1820.08 the second year. The balance at the end of the second year is $34,713.65.

4

Sinking Funds With Changing Deposits And Interest Rates

Future Value and Interest Earned

Sinking funds are occasionally established where either the deposit amount or the interest rate, or both, change. This program will compute the interest earned and the sinking fund balance for single or multiple deposits.

The procedure for entering this program is shown in the following example. Refer to the "Programming Keys" section of chapter 1 for additional information on programming procedures.

Variable Payment Sinking Fund Program

Step	Keystroke	Key Code	Step	Keystroke	Key Code
	2nd CP		07	1	01
	LRN		08	CPT	12
00	STO	61	09	2nd Bal	28
01	1	01	10	2nd Print	99
02	CPT	12	11	PV	24
03	2nd Acc	27	12	R/S	13
04	2nd Print	99	13	2nd RST	37
05	R/S	13		LRN	
06	RCL	71		2nd RST	

Make sure that the deposit amount and interest rate remain constant for the number of deposits entered before pressing R/S. Also, the value entered for %i must be the interest rate per payment period. This program can also be used for preparing a schedule of interest earned where deposits and interest remain constant. After entering the deposit amount and interest rate, simply enter one and press R/S for each period. This program assumes end of period deposits.

Example: A sinking fund is established with an initial deposit of $20,000. The first semi-annual deposit is due six months later. For the first three years, $5,000 deposits are made with 7% annual interest and semi-annual compounding. For the following five years, the deposit is $7,500 with an annual rate of 10%. The final two years' deposits are $10,000 with an annual rate of 12%.

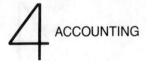

ACCOUNTING

What is the interest earned and the final balance after each
group of the deposits? (Assume semi-annual deposits and
compounding.)

Procedure	Press	Display
1. Clear calculator and mode registers; select two decimal places.	ON/c 2nd CLmode 2nd Fix 2	0.00
2. Press 2nd **Mode** until the "FIN" indicator is displayed.	2nd **Mode**	0.00
3. Enter variable payment sinking fund program as listed on previous page.		
4. Reset program.	2nd RST	0.00
5. Enter amount of initial balance or deposit (enter zero if none).	20000 PV	20000.00
6. Compute interest earned and balance for first group of payments.		
a. Calculate and enter periodic interest rate.	7 ÷ 2 = %i	3.50
b. Enter deposit as a negative value.	5000 +/− PMT	− 5000.00
c. Enter number of deposits and compute interest earned.	3 X 2 = R/S	7335.87
d. Compute balance.	R/S	57335.87 (continued)

(continued)

Procedure	Press	Display
7. Compute interest earned and balance for second group.		
a. Enter interest rate per payment period if different.	10 ÷ 2 = %i	5.00
b. Enter deposit as a negative value if different.	7500 +/− PMT	−7500.00
c. Enter number of deposits and compute interest earned.	5 × 2 = R/S	55392.41
d. Compute balance.	R/S	187728.28
8. Compute interest earned and balance for the third group.		
a. Enter interest rate if different.	12 ÷ 2 = %i	6.00
b. Enter deposit as a negative value if different.	10000 +/− PMT	−10000.00
c. Enter number of deposits and compute interest.	2 × 2 = R/S	53020.51
d. Compute balance.	R/S	280748.79

The interest earned and the final balance after each group of deposits is as follows:

Deposit Group	Interest Earned	Balance
1	7,335.87	57,335.87
2	55,392.41	187,728.28
3	53,020.51	280,748.79

5 MORTGAGES

MORTGAGES 5

This chapter explains a number of current techniques employed for home financing. The traditional long-term, level-payment mortgage is described first. This topic includes mortgage refinancing, yield when points are paid, mortgage balance, and mortgage amortization. Mortgages with balloon payments are discussed in depth including determination of monthly payment and yield with points.

A number of the newer "creative financing" type mortgages are described including variable rate mortgages, i.e., solving for the payment when the interest rate changes and solving for the yield paid. Two types of "Buy Down" mortgages, regular and graduated, are discussed. You will learn how to compute the payment schedule, and the yield on a graduated payment mortgage. You will also learn how to compute a payment schedule for level principal payment mortgage.

Wrap around mortgages are the last type of mortgage discussed in the chapter. You are shown how to compute the yield for simple and complex wraps. The chapter concludes with a program you can use for amortizing ordinary mortgages and graduated payment mortgages. Unless otherwise stated, all payments in this chapter are assumed to occur at the end of each payment period.

Ordinary Mortgages

The traditional level-payment mortgage has a fixed number of equal payments. This section shows you how to analyze this type of mortgage, often called a regular mortgage.

Monthly Payment for Home Mortgage

You are buying a $57,500 house. You plan to make a $5,800 down payment and finance the rest at 11.75% annual interest for 30 years. Excluding taxes and insurance, how much are your monthly payments on the loan? If taxes and insurance average 30% of your loan payment each month, how much is your total house payment?

	Procedure	Press	Display
1.	Clear calculator and mode registers; select two decimal places.	[ON/c] [2nd] **CLmode** [2nd] **Fix** 2	0.00
2.	Press [2nd] **Mode** until the "FIN" indicator is displayed.	[2nd] **Mode**	0.00
3.	Calculate and enter number of payments.	30 [X] 12 [=] [N]	360.00
4.	Calculate and enter periodic interest rate.	11.75 [÷] 12 [=] [%i]	0.98
5.	Calculate and enter loan amount (cost of house minus down payment).	57500 [−] 5800 [=] [PV]	51700.00
6.	Compute monthly payment.	[CPT] [PMT]	521.86
7.	Add estimated taxes and insurance to calculate monthly house payment.	[+] 30 [%] [=]	678.42

The monthly payments on the loan are $521.86, and the total monthly house payments are $678.42.

Loan Amount a Buyer Can Afford

A loan company usually finances a house if the potential monthly payment does not exceed 25% of a buyer's gross income. Assume you have a gross monthly income of $2,700. What price house can you afford to finance at a 12% annual interest rate for 30 years with 15% down? Monthly taxes and insurance are 30% of the loan payment.

If the memory indicator does not show at least one data memory available, press [2nd] CP before entering the solution.

Procedure	Press	Display
1. Clear calculator and mode registers; select two decimal places.	[ON/C][2nd] **CLmode** [2nd] **Fix** 2	0.00
2. Press [2nd] **Mode** until the "FIN" indicator is displayed.	[2nd] **Mode**	0.00
3. Calculate and enter number of monthly payments.	30 [X] 12 [=][N]	360.00
4. Calculate and enter periodic interest rate.	12 [÷] 12 [=][%i]	1.00
5. Calculate and store maximum allowable payment.	2700 [X] 25 [%][=][STO] 1	675.00
6. Calculate and enter maximum allowable loan payment.	1 [+] 30 [%][=] [1/x][X][RCL] 1 [=][PMT]	519.23
7. Compute and store maximum allowable loan amount.	[CPT][PV][STO] 1	50478.75
8. Calculate affordable house price.	1 [−] 15 [%][=][1/x] [X][RCL] 1 [=]	59386.76
9. Calculate down payment.	[−][RCL] 1 [=]	8908.01

You can afford to finance a $59,386 house, and your down payment will be $8,908.

Time Required to Pay Off a Mortgage

The monthly payments for the mortgage on your house are $384.46 (excluding taxes and insurance). The annual interest rate is 8.5% compounded monthly. In the past, you have made extra principal payments so that your current loan balance is $44,612.57. How many payments remain if you make the regular $384.46 payment each month? What happens if you pay $400 each month?

If the memory indicator does not show at least one data memory available, press [2nd] CP before entering the solution.

	Procedure	Press	Display
1.	Clear calculator and mode registers; select two decimal places.	[ON/c] [2nd] **CLmode** [2nd] **Fix** 2	0.00
2.	Press [2nd] **Mode** until the "FIN" indicator is displayed.	[2nd] **Mode**	0.00
3.	Enter periodic interest rate.	8.5 [÷] 12 [=] [%i]	0.71
4.	Enter current loan balance.	44612.57 [PV]	44612.57
5.	Enter required monthly payment.	384.46 [PMT]	384.46
6.	Compute number of payments.	[CPT] [N] [STO] 1	244.49
7.	Enter increased payment and compute number of payments.	400 [PMT] [CPT] [N]	221.12
8.	Calculate difference.	[+/−] [+] [RCL] 1 [=]	23.37

If you make regular monthly payments of $384.46, there will be approximately 245 payments remaining. By increasing the amount of your monthly payments to $400, you can reduce the term of the loan by approximately 23 payments or almost two years.

MORTGAGES

Monthly Payments After Refinancing a Mortgage

Assume that 210 payments of $813.69 each remain on your current mortgage. The unpaid balance is $65,425.33. The current annual interest rate is 13.5% compounded monthly. You can refinance the mortgage at a rate of 10% compounded monthly. How much will your monthly payment be if you refinance the mortgage over the remaining 210 payments?

Procedure	Press	Display
1. Clear calculator and mode registers; select two decimal places.	[ON/c] [2nd] CLmode [2nd] Fix 2	0.00
2. Press [2nd] **Mode** until the "FIN" indicator is displayed.	[2nd] **Mode**	0.00
3. Enter number of monthly payments.	210 [N]	210.00
4. Calculate and enter new periodic interest rate.	10 [÷] 12 [=] [%i]	0.83
5. Enter amount to be refinanced.	65425.33 [PV]	65425.33
6. Compute amount of new payment.	[CPT] [PMT]	660.89

Your new monthly payment will be $660.89.

Determining Points on a Loan

Loans are often made where the stated interest rate is below the market yield. Lenders achieve the market yield by charging a cash fee usually called points. Points are charged for a number of reasons such as usury laws, or other business reasons. Points are usually expressed as percentages so two points are two percent of the amount borrowed. Computing points requires two steps. First, find the present value of the cash flows using the yield rate. Second, subtract the present value from the amount borrowed to determine the points in dollars. The percentage points are determined by dividing the mortgage amount into the dollar points and multiplying by 100. The following example illustrates how to calculate points.

Example: A customer has asked your company to lend her $120,000. She wants the loan payment calculated using a thirty year amortization schedule but agrees to pay off the loan at the end of ten years. She wants a stated interest rate of 12% annually compounded monthly and will pay points on the loan. If the market yield rate on mortgages is 14% annually with monthly compounding, how many points will she pay? Also, if the yield is an annual effective rate of 14%, how many points are paid?

If the memory indicator does not display at least one data memory available, press [2nd] **CP** before entering the solution.

	Procedure	Press	Display
1.	Clear calculator and mode registers; select two decimal places.	[ON/C][2nd] **CLmode** [2nd] **Fix 2**	**0.00**
2.	Press [2nd] **Mode** until the "FIN" indicator is displayed.	[2nd] **Mode**	**0.00**
3.	Compute scheduled payments.		
	a. Calculate and enter periodic interest rate.	12 [÷] 12 [=][%i]	**1.00**
	b. Enter number of payments for loan amortization.	30 [X] 12 [=][N]	**360.00**
	c. Enter amount borrowed and store.	120000 [PV] [STO] 1	**120000.00**
	d. Compute periodic payment.	[CPT][PMT]	**1234.34**
	e. Enter number of scheduled payments.	10 [X] 12 [=][N]	**120.00**
	f. Compute payoff amount after last payment.	[CPT][FV]	**112101.59**
4.	Compute points for annual nominal yield.		
	a. Enter desired annual nominal yield and divide by number of payments per year.	14 [÷] 12 [=][%i]	**1.17**
	b. Compute present value of payments.	[CPT][PV]	**107366.71**
	c. Subtract amount in step b from loan amount to determine dollar amount of points.	[+/-][+][RCL] 1 [=]	**12633.29**
	d. Calculate percentage points.	[÷][RCL] 1 [X] 100 [=]	**10.53**

(continued)

(continued)

Procedure	Press	Display
5. Compute points for annual effective yield.		
a. Enter number of payments per year.	12 `◄EFF`	**12.00**
b. Enter annual effective rate and convert to annual nominal rate.	14 `=`	**13.17**
c. Divide by number of payments per year.	`÷` 12 `=` `%i`	**1.10**
d. Compute present value.	`CPT` `PV`	**112340.28**
e. Calculate dollar amount of points.	`+/−` `+` `RCL` 1 `=`	**7659.72**
f. Calculate percentage points.	`÷` `RCL` 1 `X` 100 `=`	**6.38**

To earn an annual yield of 14% compounded monthly requires 10.53 points. To earn a 14% annual effective yield, however, requires only 6.38 points since the 14% annual nominal rate is equivalent to an annual effective rate of 14.93%

Actual Interest Rate (Yield) Paid When Buyer Pays Points

Joe recently borrowed $76,000 for 30 years to purchase his dream home. His monthly payments of $774.44 are based on an annual interest rate of 11-7/8% compounded monthly. Joe had to pay three points to borrow the money. Thus, Joe only received $73,720 (97% of $76,000), but he must repay the full actual mortgage amount and pay interest on the full amount. What is the annual nominal interest rate (yield) compounded monthly, and the annual effective rate for Joe's mortgage?

If the memory indicator does not show at least one data memory available, press [2nd] CP before entering the solution.

Procedure	Press	Display
1. Clear calculator and mode registers; select two decimal places.	[ON/C] [2nd] **CLmode** [2nd] **Fix 2**	0.00
2. Press [2nd] **Mode** until the "FIN" indicator is displayed.	[2nd] **Mode**	0.00
3. Enter number of payments.	30 [×] 12 [=] [N]	360.00
4. Enter monthly payment.	774.44 [PMT]	774.44
5. Subtract points from amount borrowed and enter as present value.	76000 [−] 3 [%] [=] [PV]	73720.00
6. Compute interest rate per payment period.	[CPT] [%i]	1.02
7. Multiply by number of payments per year for annual nominal interest rate and store.	[×] 12 [=] [STO] 1	12.28
8. Enter number of payments per year and compute annual effective rate.	12 [APR▶] [RCL] 1 [=]	13.00

Joe paid an annual nominal rate of 12.28% which is equivalent to an annual effective rate of 13%.

Actual Interest Rate (Yield) Paid When a Mortgage is Paid Off Early

Joe borrowed $76,000 for thirty years to purchase a house. His monthly payments of $774.44 are based on an annual interest rate of 11-7/8% compounded monthly. Joe paid three points to borrow the money. After ten years, Joe sells the house. The remaining balance on the mortgage is $70,894.68. However, he must pay a penalty of $4,108.41 because he is paying the loan off early. What is the actual annual nominal interest rate (yield) and the annual effective rate Joe paid on his mortgage?

If the memory indicator does not show at least one data memory available, press [2nd] **CP** before entering the solution.

Procedure	Press	Display
1. Clear calculator and mode registers; select two decimal places.	ON/c 2nd CLmode 2nd Fix 2	0.00
2. Press 2nd Mode until the "FIN" indicator is displayed.	2nd Mode	0.00
3. Enter number of payments made.	10 ✕ 12 = N	120.00
4. Enter payment amount.	774.44 PMT	774.44
5. Subtract points from amount borrowed and enter as present value.	76000 − 3 % = PV	73720.00
6. Add early payoff penalty to loan balance and enter.	70894.68 + 4198.41 = FV	75093.09
7. Compute periodic interest rate.	CPT %i	1.06
8. Multiply by number of payments per year to obtain annual nominal interest rate; store results.	✕ 12 = STO 1	12.70
9. Enter number of payments per year and calculate annual effective interest rate.	12 APR▶ RCL 1 =	13.47

While the loan's APR is 11-7/8%, Joe really paid an annual nominal rate (yield) of 12.70% or an annual effective rate of 13.47% after points and the early pay-off penalty.

Balance Owed, Principal, and Interest Paid at the End of a Specified Time on a Mortgage

You borrowed $32,000 to buy your house and have lived in it for nine years. Your monthly loan payments (not including taxes and insurance) are $299.72. Your mortgage carries 8.5% annual interest, compounded monthly. How much interest have you paid? How much of the loan have you paid off? How much interest did you pay during the ninth year?

If the memory indicator does not show at least one data memory available, press [2nd] CP before entering the solution.

Procedure	Press	Display
1. Clear calculator and mode registers; select two decimal places.	[ON/c] [2nd] **CLmode** [2nd] **Fix** 2	0.00
2. Press [2nd] **Mode** until the "FIN" indicator is displayed.	[2nd] **Mode**	0.00
3. Calculate and enter periodic interest rate.	8.5 [÷] 12 [=] [%i]	0.71
4. Enter monthly payment.	299.72 [PMT]	299.72
5. Enter original loan amount.	32000 [PV]	32000.00
6. Compute and store interest paid over time period (nine years).	9 [X] 12 [=] [CPT] [2nd] **Acc** [STO] 1	20579.40
7. Compute remaining balance on mortgage after nine years.	108 [CPT] [2nd] **Bal**	20209.64
8. Subtract remaining balance from original loan amount of principal paid.	[+/−] [+] [RCL] [PV] [=]	11790.36
9. Compute interest paid for eight years.	8 [X] 12 [=] [CPT] [2nd] **Acc**	18777.86
10. Subtract interest paid for eight years from interest paid for nine years to calculate interest paid during ninth year.	[+/−] [+] [RCL] 1 [=]	1801.54

Assuming that all payments made were $299.72, you have paid $20,579.40 in interest and $11,790.36 in principal on the loan. The interest paid during the ninth year was $1,801.54.

How Much of a Given Payment on a Home Is Principal and How Much Is Interest

Assume that you have made 85 scheduled payments on your home. Your original loan was for $32,000 with an 8.5% interest rate. Your payments (less taxes and insurance) are $250 per month. You would like to know how much of your next two loan payments will be interest and how much will be added to your equity (the amount of your loan that is paid off).

Procedure	Press	Display
1. Clear calculator and mode registers; select two decimal places.	[ON/c] [2nd] **CLmode** [2nd] **Fix 2**	0.00
2. Press [2nd] **Mode** until the "FIN" indicator is displayed.	[2nd] **Mode**	0.00
3. Calculate and enter periodic interest rate.	8.5 [÷] 12 [=] [%i]	0.71
4. Enter original loan amount.	32000 [PV]	32000.00
5. Enter payment amount.	250 [PMT]	250.00
6. Enter number of payment and calculate amount that applies to principal.	86 [CPT] [2nd] P/I	42.51
7. Display interest amount of 86th payment.	[x:y]	207.49
8. Repeat steps six and seven for payment number 87.	87 [CPT] [2nd] P/I [x:y]	42.82 207.18

For payment number 86, the principal is $42.51 and the interest is $207.49. For payment number 87, the principal is $42.82 and the interest is $207.18.

Mortgages With Balloon Payments Or Early Payoff

Some mortgages are made where a large final payment is due in addition to the last regular payment. This final payment is called a "balloon" payment. Your calculator always assumes the balloon occurs at the end of the final regular payment periods and is separate from the regular payment. A balloon payment is one which is made at the end of a series of regular payments. The balloon may be larger or smaller than the regular payment and can be used to pay off a loan before its normal duration is complete.

Determining the Monthly Payment

You are considering buying a lake house that requires a $15,000 mortgage, but you want the payments to be as small as possible. You know that you'll receive $3,000 from an insurance policy in 14 years and would like that money to be a balloon payment on the lake house mortgage. If the 14-year mortgage (including the balloon payment) is set at 9.25% annual interest, compounded monthly, what is your monthly payment with and without the balloon payment?

Procedure	Press	Display
1. Clear calculator and mode registers; select two decimal places.	ON/c 2nd **CLmode** 2nd **Fix 2**	0.00
2. Press 2nd **Mode** until the "FIN" indicator is displayed.	2nd **Mode**	0.00
3. Enter number of regular payments.	14 X 12 = N	168.00
4. Calculate and enter periodic interest rate.	9.25 ÷ 12 = %i	0.77
5. Enter amount of mortgage.	15000 PV	15000.00
6. Enter amount of balloon.	3000 FV	3000.00
7. Compute monthly payment with balloon.	CPT PMT	150.76
8. Enter zero for future value.	0 FV	0.00
9. Compute monthly payment without a balloon.	CPT PMT	159.54

The monthly payment is $150.76 with the $3,000 balloon and
$159.54 without the balloon.

Finding the Interest Rate (Yield) When the Buyer Pays Points

Assume that you want to borrow $80,000 for 15 years with a
monthly payment of $853.81 and a final balloon payment of
$69,271.11 after the last monthly payment. The stated annual
interest rate is 12.5% compounded monthly. However, you
must pay four points to obtain the loan. In other words, you
are actually borrowing $76,800 (96% of $80,000) and repaying
$80,000. What is the actual annual interest rate (yield), com-
pounded monthly, that you pay for this mortgage and the
annual effective rate?

If the memory indicator does not display at least one data memory available, press 2nd CP before entering the solution.

Procedure	Press	Display
1. Clear calculator and mode registers; select two decimal places.	ON/c 2nd CLmode 2nd Fix 2	0.00
2. Press 2nd Mode until the "FIN" indicator is displayed.	2nd Mode	0.00
3. Enter number of monthly payments.	15 X 12 = N	180.00
4. Calculate and store cash received (loan amount minus points).	80000 − 4 % = PV	76800.00
5. Enter monthly payment.	853.81 PMT	853.81
6. Enter balloon.	69271.11 FV	69271.11
7. Compute monthly interest rate.	CPT %i	1.09
8. Multiply by number of payments per year to obtain annual nominal interest rate.	X 12 = STO 1	13.13
9. Enter number of payments per year and calculate annual effective interest rate.	12 APR▶ RCL 1 =	13.95

The annual nominal interest rate (yield) compounded monthly is 13.13% and the annual effective rate is 13.95%.

Calculating the Balloon Payment Needed to Pay Off a Loan

It is sometimes advantageous to pay off a loan with a balloon payment before the scheduled termination of the mortgage. The following procedure calculates the size of balloon payment needed for early payoff of a mortgage, assuming that the scheduled payment has been made each month.

Consider a mortgage balance of $250,000 that is to terminate in 25 years. If the annual interest rate is 10-1/2%, compounded monthly, what balloon payment must be made in 15 years to pay off the loan? The balloon payment, in this case, is the balance remaining on the mortgage after 15 years.

	Procedure	Press	Display
1.	Clear calculator and mode registers; select two decimal places.	ON/c 2nd **CLmode** 2nd **Fix 2**	0.00
2.	Press 2nd **Mode** until the "FIN" indicator is displayed.	2nd **Mode**	0.00
3.	Enter number of scheduled payments.	25 ✕ 12 = N	300.00
4.	Calculate and enter periodic interest rate.	10.5 ÷ 12 = %i	0.88
5.	Enter amount of mortgage.	250000 PV	250000.00
6.	Compute monthly payment.	CPT PMT	2360.45
7.	Enter amount of payment rounded to nearest cent.*	2360.45 PMT	2360.45
8.	Enter number of payments you will have made at end of 15th year.	15 ✕ 12 =	180.00
9.	Calculate balloon payment.	CPT 2nd **Bal**	174934.55

*Although the display in step six shows the payment amount rounded to two decimal places, the calculator uses all internal digits (up to 11) for subsequent calculations. For proper results, the payment amount must be rounded to two decimal places and then entered in step seven since payments must be in dollars and cents.

Mortgages With Balloon Payments Or Early Payoff

Determining the Loan Amount a Buyer Can Afford

You are considering a 20-year mortgage with an annual interest rate of 12.75% compounded monthly and a final balloon payment of $25,000. If you can pay $850 per month for principal and interest, how much can you borrow? (Note: Since payments occur at the end of each period, this is an ordinary annuity situation.)

	Procedure	Press	Display
1.	Clear calculator and mode registers; select two decimal places.	ON/c 2nd CLmode 2nd Fix 2	0.00
2.	Press 2nd Mode until the "FIN" indicator is displayed.	2nd Mode	0.00
3.	Enter number of monthly payments.	20 X 12 = N	240.00
4.	Calculate and enter periodic interest rate.	12.75 ÷ 12 = %i	1.06
5.	Enter amount of monthly payment.	850 PMT	850.00
6.	Enter balloon payment.	25000 FV	25000.00
7.	Compute total amount you can borrow (present value).	CPT PV	75647.35

You can borrow $75,647.35.

Canadian Mortgages

MORTGAGES

Some Canadian mortgages require monthly payments with interest compounded semi-annually instead of monthly. Also, the mortgages are usually refinanced at the end of a fixed period of time such as five years. The procedure is the same for the mortgages previously discussed. The following example shows you how to use semi-annual compounding on your calculator.

Solving for the Payment and Remaining Balance

You borrow $60,000 for 20 years at an annual interest rate of 13% compounded semi-annually. How much is the payment and the amount necessary to pay off the mortgage after five years?

If the memory indicator does not show at least one data memory available, press [2nd] CP before entering the solution.

Procedure	Press	Display
1. Clear calculator and mode registers; select two decimal places.	[ON/C] [2nd] CLmode [2nd] Fix 2	0.00
2. Press [2nd] Mode until the "FIN" indicator is displayed.	[2nd] Mode	0.00
3. Convert semi-annual interest to equivalent monthly rate.		
a. Convert semi-annual interest to equivalent annual effective rate.	2 [APR▶] 13 [=] [STO] 1	13.42
b. Convert annual effective rate to annual nominal rate with monthly compounding.	12 [◀EFF] [RCL] 1 [=]	12.66
c. Divide by number of payments per year and enter.	[÷] 12 [=] [%i]	1.06

(continued)

(continued)

Procedure	Press	Display
4. Calculate and enter number of payments.	20 ⊠ 12 ⊜ N	**240.00**
5. Enter amount borrowed.	60000 PV	**60000.00**
6. Compute monthly payment.	CPT PMT	**688.52**

Solve for Balance After Five Years.

7. Enter payment to nearest penny.*	688.52 PMT	**688.52**
8. Calculate number of payments made.	5 ⊠ 12 ⊜	**60.00**
9. Compute balance after five years.	CPT 2nd **Bal**	**55389.84**

The monthly payment is $688.52, and $55,389.84 is required to pay off the mortgage after five years. The 13% semi-annual rate is equal to a 12.66% annual rate with monthly compounding.

*Although the display in step six shows the payment amount rounded to two decimal places, the calculator uses all internal digits (up to 11) for subsequent calculations. For proper results, the payment amount must be rounded to two decimal places and then entered in step seven since payments must be in dollars and cents.

Some mortgages now have provisions for changing the
interest rate periodically to reflect changes in the cost of
money in the market. A new payment amount is calculated
and the number of remaining payments remains constant.

Determining the Payment When Interest Rate Changes

Jackie borrowed $35,000 for 30 years to purchase a summer
vacation house. The mortgage is for 30 years at an annual
interest rate compounded monthly of 11.5% with monthly
payments of $346.60. The mortgages contained a provision
that as the cost of money changes, the interest rate can be
adjusted. After two years, the annual interest rate with
monthly compounding increased to 12.5%. What is the
amount of the new payment?

Variable Rate Mortgages

Procedure	Press	Display
1. Clear calculator and mode registers; select two decimal places.	[ON/c] [2nd] **CLmode** [2nd] **Fix** 2	**0.00**
2. Press [2nd] **Mode** until the "FIN" indicator is displayed.	[2nd] **Mode**	**0.00**
3. Enter loan amount for current payment.	35000 [PV]	**35000.00**
4. Calculate and enter periodic interest rate for current payment.	11.5 [÷] 12 [=] [%i]	**0.96**
5. Enter amount of current payment.	346.60 [PMT]	**346.60**
6. Enter number of payments made for amount shown in step five.	2 [×] 12 [=]	**24.00**
7. Compute balance and enter as present value.	[CPT] [2nd] **Bal** [PV]	**34699.83**
8. Enter remaining number of payments.	360 [−] 24 [=] [N]	**336.00**
9. Calculate and enter new interest rate per month.	12.5 [÷] 12 [=] [%i]	**1.04**
10. Compute new monthly payment.	[CPT] [PMT]	**372.92**

The new payment is $372.92.

Determining the Annual Interest Rate (Yield) Paid

Your uncle borrowed $60,000 for 30 years to purchase his
house. The mortgage was originally established using a 9%
annual interest rate with monthly compounding. The loan
allowed the mortgage rate to be adjusted as interest rates
change. As a result, your uncle made 36 payments of $482.77,
12 payments of $545.64, and 18 payments of $566.78 before
paying off the loan balance of $57,602.53. What was the
average annual interest with monthly compounding and the
annual effective rate paid on the mortgage? (Note: Since
payments vary, this is a variable/grouped cash flow situation.)

Procedure	Press	Display
1. Clear calculator and mode registers; select two decimal places.	ON/C 2nd CLmode 2nd Fix 2	0.00
2. Press 2nd **Mode** until the "CF" indicator is displayed.	2nd **Mode**	0.00
3. Enter amount borrowed.	60000 +/- PV	−60000.00
4. Enter first group of payments.		
a. Amount.	482.77	482.77
b. Number.	2nd Frq 36	Fr 036
c. Store.	STO 1	482.77
5. Enter second group.		
a. Amount.	545.64	545.64
b. Number.	2nd Frq 12	Fr 012
c. Store.	STO 2	545.64
Payment in final group.		
a. Amount.	566.78	566.78
b. Number.	2nd Frq 17	Fr 017
c. Store.	STO 3	566.78

(continued)

(continued)

Procedure	Press	Display
6. Add last payment to pay off amount and store as last group.	566.78 $\boxed{+}$ 57602.53 $\boxed{=}$ $\boxed{\text{STO}}$ 4	**58169.31**
7. Compute monthly interest rate.	$\boxed{\text{CPT}}$ $\boxed{\text{2nd}}$ **IRR**	**0.81**
8. Multiply by number of payments per year to determine annual rate with monthly compounding.	$\boxed{\times}$ 12 $\boxed{=}$ $\boxed{\%i}$	**9.69**
9. Enter number of payments per year and calculate annual effective rate.	12 $\boxed{\text{APR}\blacktriangleright}$ $\boxed{\text{RCL}}$ $\boxed{\%i}$ $\boxed{=}$	**10.13**

For the time your uncle made payments, his average annual interest rate with monthly compounding is 9.69% or an effective annual rate of 10.13%.

"Buy Down" Mortgages

5 MORTGAGES

Determining the Payments for a Simple "Buy Down"

Some lenders offer a "Buy Down" mortgage. With this type mortgage, the seller subsidizes the borrower's mortgage payments by depositing a lump amount in an escrow account paying interest. The difference between the borrower's monthly payments and the actual monthly payments is taken from the escrow account each month. The subsidy's time period usually ranges from one to three years. At the end of the subsidy period, the borrower assumes responsibility for the full payment.

Example: Joe has just borrowed $50,000 to purchase a house. The mortgage has a 30 year term and a 15-1/2% annual interest rate compounded monthly. The seller, however, places an amount in escrow that reduces Joe's loan to a 12.5% interest rate for the the first three years. What is the payment Joe makes for the first three years and the revised payment for the remaining mortgage term? Also, what is the subsidy amount the seller must place in escrow assuming a 6% annual rate compounded monthly?

If the memory indicator does not display at least one data memory available, press ⟮2nd⟯ CP before entering the solution.

	Procedure	Press	Display
1.	Clear calculator and mode register; select two decimal places.	ON/c 2nd CLmode 2nd Fix 2	0.00
2.	Press 2nd Mode until the "FIN" indicator is displayed.	2nd Mode	0.00
3.	Enter total number of payments.	30 X 12 = N	360.00
4.	Enter amount borrowed.	50000 PV	50000.00
5.	Calculate and enter *actual* monthly loan rate.	15.5 ÷ 12 = %i	1.29
6.	Compute total payment and store.	CPT PMT STO 1	652.26
7.	Enter monthly subsidized loan rate.	12.5 ÷ 12 = %i	1.04
8.	Compute subsidized payment.	CPT PMT	533.63
9.	Compute difference in payments and enter monthly subsidy.	+/− + RCL 1 = PMT	118.63
10.	Enter number of subsidized payments and calculate total amount.	X 36 =	4270.66
11.	Enter savings account interest rate per month.	6 ÷ 12 = %i	0.50
12.	Enter number of subsidized payments.	36 N	36.00
13.	Compute amount to be deposited in savings account.	CPT PV	3899.47

Joe makes 36 payments of $533.63 and the remaining payments are $652.26. The lender deposits $4,270.66 in escrow if no interest is earned, or $3,899.47 if interest is earned at 6% annual compounded monthly.

"Buy Down" Mortgages

5 MORTGAGES

Determining the Payments for a Graduated "Buy Down"

With a graduated "Buy Down" mortgage, the borrower's payments increase each year. The seller places in escrow an amount that covers the difference between the full payment and the subsidized payment.

Example: Ann has borrowed $50,000 to purchase her house. The 30-year loan has a 14.25% annual interest rate with monthly compounding. The seller agrees to place in escrow an amount which will reduce her interest rate to 11.25% the first year, 12.25% the second year, and 13.25% the third year. She assumes the full payment after the third year. What is Ann's payment schedule and the amount the seller must place in an escrow savings account paying 5-3/4% annual interest compounded monthly? (Note: Since payments vary this is a variable/grouped cash flow situation.)

If the memory indicator does not display at least three data memories available, press [2nd] CP before entering the solution.

Procedure	Press	Display
1. Clear calculator and mode registers; select two decimal places.	[ON/c] [2nd] CLmode [2nd] Fix 2	0.00
2. Press [2nd] Mode until the "FIN" indicator is displayed.	[2nd] Mode	0.00
3. Enter total number of payments.	30 [×] 12 [=] [N]	360.00
4. Enter amount borrowed.	50000 [PV]	50000.00
5. Calculate and enter actual loan rate per month.	14.25 [÷] 12 [=] [%i]	1.19
6. Compute total monthly payment and store.	[CPT] [PMT] [STO] 1	602.34

(continued)

(continued)

Procedure	Press	Display
7. Compute loan balance at end of:		
a. Year one.	12 [CPT] [2nd] **Bal**	
	[STO] 2	**49889.87**
b. Year two.	24 [CPT] [2nd] **Bal**	
	[STO] 3	**49762.98**
First year's subsidy.		
8. Enter first year's monthly subsidized rate.	11.25 [÷] 12 [=] [%i]	**0.94**
9. Compute subsidized payment.	[CPT] [PMT]	**485.63**
10. Compute monthly subsidy for first year.	[+/−] [+] [RCL] 1 [=]	**116.71**
Second year's subsidy.		
11. Enter second year's monthly subsidized rate.	12.25 [÷] 12 [=] [%i]	**1.02**
12. Enter number of remaining payments.	[RCL] [N] [−] 12 [=] [N]	**348.00**
13. Enter loan balance at end of year one.	[RCL] 2 [PV]	**49889.87**
14. Compute second year's payments.	[CPT] [PMT]	**524.60**
15. Compute monthly subsidy for second year.	[+/−] [+] [RCL] 1 [=]	**77.75**
Third year's subsidy.		
16. Enter third year's monthly subsidized rate.	13.25 [÷] 12 [=] [%i]	**1.10**
17. Enter number of remaining payments.	[RCL] [N] [−] 12 [=] [N]	**336.00**
18. Enter loan balance.	[RCL] 3 [PV]	**49762.98**
19. Compute third year's monthly payments.	[CPT] [PMT]	**563.54**

(continued)

(continued)

Procedure	Press	Display
20. Compute monthly subsidy for third year.	+/− + RCL 1	
	=	**38.80**

Present value of subsidy payments.

Procedure	Press	Display
21. Press 2nd **Mode** until the "CF" indicator is displayed.	2nd **Mode**	**38.80**
22. Enter savings account rate per month.	5.75 ÷ 12	
	= %i	**0.48**
23. Enter first year's subsidy payments.		
a. Amount.	116.71	**116.71**
b. Number.	2nd **Frq** 12	**Fr 012**
c. Store.	STO 1	**116.71**
24. Enter second year's subsidy payments.		
a. Amount.	77.75	**77.75**
b. Number.	2nd **Frq** 12	**Fr 012**
c. Store.	STO 2	**77.75**
25. Enter third year's subsidy payments.		
a. Amount.	38.80	**38.80**
b. Number.	2nd **Frq** 12	**Fr 012**
c. Store.	STO 3	**38.80**
26. Compute amount to deposit in savings account to subsidize loan.	CPT 2nd **NPV**	**2614.50**

Ann makes monthly payments of $485.63 the first year, $524.60 the second year, and $563.54 the third year. Starting with the fourth year, her payments remain constant at $602.34 per month. The seller must deposit $2,614.50 in an account paying 5.75% annual interest compounded monthly to cover the monthly subsidy payments.

Graduated Payment Mortgages

Mortgages that have payments increasing at the end of each year for a number of years are called Graduated Payment Mortgages (GPM's). These mortgages often have the monthly payment increasing by 5% at the end of years two through six with constant payments for years seven through 30.

Unlike regular mortgages, GPM's early payments do not cover interest. As a result, the loan balance increases until the monthly payments exceed monthly interest. For tax-payers on a "cash basis", only the interest actually paid is deductible. The difference between the interest paid and the interest accrued on the mortgage is added to the loan balance.

This section shows you how to solve for GPM's initial payment, yield, and amortization schedule.

Solving for Payment Schedule

Sam has a $40,000, 30-year graduated payment mortgage with 12.5% annual nominal interest compounded monthly. After the first year, the monthly payments increase by 5% per year for five years, i.e., the payments in year two are 5% higher than in year one, and year three payments are 5% higher than in year two. These annual increases stop after the increase in year six. As a result, the final 300 payments remain constant. What is Sam's payment schedule?

Your calculator will not solve directly for the payment amount for a GPM, but the keystroke procedure shown below computes the initial payment and remaining payment amounts.

Reference: Greynolds, Aronofsky, and Frame, *Financial Analysis Using Calculators: Time Value of Money.*

MORTGAGES

If the memory indicator does not display at least four data memories available, press [2nd] **CP** before entering the solution.

Procedure	Press	Display
1. Clear calculator and mode registers; select two decimal places.	[ON/c] [2nd] **CLmode** [2nd] **Fix 2**	0.00
2. Press [2nd] **Mode** until the "FIN" indicator is displayed.	[2nd] **Mode**	0.00
3. Enter interest per month, calculate and store results.	12.5 [÷] 12 [=] [%i] [%] [+] 1 [2nd] y^x 12 [=] [STO] 1	1.13
4. Enter percentage amount payments increase.	5 [%] [+] 1 [÷] [RCL] 1 [=] [STO] 1	0.93
5. Enter number of years payments increase by amount entered in step four. Calculate and store results.	[2nd] y^x 5 [=] [STO] 2	0.69
6. Enter number of years for which payments change and total payments. Calculate number of constant payments.	5 [×] 12 [+/−] [+] 360 [=] [N]	300.00
7. Enter one for payment, calculate and store results.	1 [PMT] [CPT] [PV] [×] [RCL] 2 [=] [STO] 3	62.86
8. Calculate following values.	[RCL] 1 [−] 1 [=] [STO] 1 [RCL] 2 [−] 1 [÷] [RCL] 1 [=] [STO] 4	4.32

(continued)

Graduated Payment Mortgages

(continued)

Procedure	Press	Display
9. Enter number of payments per year and calculate following values.	12 [N] [CPT] [PV] [X] [RCL] 4 [+] [RCL] 3 [=] [1/x] [X]	0.01
10. Enter loan amount and calculate first year's payments.	40000 [=]	359.11
11. Enter yearly percentage increase and compute second year's payments.	[+] 5 [%] [=]	377.06
12. Repeat step 11 for each remaining year's payments increase.		
a. Third year.	[+] 5 [%] [=]	395.92
b. Fourth year.	[+] 5 [%] [=]	415.71
c. Fifth year.	[+] 5 [%] [=]	436.50
d. Sixth year.	[+] 5 [%] [=]	458.32

Sam's scheduled payments are:

Year	Payment Amount	Number of Payments
1	$359.11	12
2	377.06	12
3	395.92	12
4	415.71	12
5	436.50	12
6 thru 30	458.32	300

Determining the Yield

Sam borrowed $40,000 for 30 years with an annual interest rate of 12.5% compounded monthly. He paid two points to obtain the mortgage. The mortgage was a graduated payment mortgage with the following schedule of payments.

Payment Amount	Number of Payments
$359.11	12
377.06	12
395.92	12
415.71	12
436.50	12
458.32	300

What is the actual nominal rate (yield) compounded monthly and the annual effective rate Sam is paying?

Comment: Use the grouped cash flow keys to enter the payments since they vary, and solve for the IRR which is the interest rate that makes the present value of the payments equal to the net cash flow from the loan.

Graduated Payment Mortgages

Procedure	Press	Display
1. Clear calculator and mode registers; select two decimal places.	[ON/c][2nd] **CLmode** [2nd] **Fix** 2	**0.00**
2. Press [2nd] **Mode** until the "CF" indicator is displayed.	[2nd] **Mode**	**0.00**
3. Subtract points from amount borrowed and enter as negative present value.	40000 [−] 2 [%][=][+/−][PV]	**−39200.00**
4. Enter first year's payments.		
a. Amount.	359.11	**359.11**
b. Number.	[2nd] **Frq** 12	**Fr 012**
c. Store.	[STO] 1	**359.11**
5. Enter second year's payments.		
a. Amount.	377.06	**377.06**
b. Number.	[2nd] **Frq** 12	**Fr 012**
c. Store.	[STO] 2	**377.06**
6. Enter third year's payments.		
a. Amount.	395.92	**395.92**
b. Number.	[2nd] **Frq** 12	**Fr 012**
c. Store.	[STO] 3	**395.92**
7. Enter fourth year's payments.		
a. Amount.	415.71	**415.71**
b. Number.	[2nd] **Frq** 12	**Fr 012**
c. Store.	[STO] 4	**415.71**
		(continued)

(continued)

Procedure	Press	Display
8. Enter fifth year's payments.		
a. Amount.	436.50	**436.50**
b. Number.	[2nd] **Frq** 12	**Fr 012**
c. Store.	[STO] 5	**436.50**
9. Enter remaining payments.		
a. Amount.	458.32	**458.32**
b. Number.	[2nd] **Frq** 300	**FR 300**
c. Store.	[STO] 6	**458.32**
10. Compute the annual monthly yield.*	[CPT][2nd] **IRR**	**1.06**
11. Multiply by number of payments per year to determine annual yield with monthly compounding; store results.	[X] 12 [=] [%i]	**12.76**
12. Enter number of payments per year and compute annual effective rate.	12 [APR▸] [RCL][%i][=]	**13.54**

With the points, the yield on Sam's mortgage is an annual
nominal rate of 12.76% or an annual effective rate of
13.54%.

*This calculation requires approximately two minutes.

Payment Schedule

Some mortgages are set up so that the amount of principal paid each period remains constant.

Comment: The total payment is equal to the level principal payment plus the interest for the period. Interest is calculated by multiplying the beginning period balance by the periodic interest rate.

The program below computes the monthly interest, total payment, and remaining balance for constant principal payment mortgages.

The procedure for entering this program is shown in the following example. Refer to the "Programming Keys" section of chapter 1 for additional information on programming procedures.

Step	Keystroke	Key Code	Step	Keystroke	Key Code
	[2nd] CP		16	[+]	85
	[LRN]		17	[RCL]	71
00	[RCL]	71	18	[PMT]	23
01	[N]	21	19	[=]	95
02	[+]	85	20	[2nd] Print	99
03	1	01	21	[R/S]	13
04	[=]	95	22	[RCL]	71
05	[N]	21	23	[PV]	24
06	[2nd] Print	99	24	[−]	75
07	[R/S]	13	25	[RCL]	71
08	[RCL]	71	26	[PMT]	23
09	[PV]	24	27	[=]	95
10	[X]	65	28	[PV]	24
11	[RCL]	71	29	[2nd] Print	99
12	[%i]	22	30	[R/S]	13
13	[=]	95	31	[2nd] RST	37
14	[2nd] Print	99		[LRN]	
15	[R/S]	13		[2nd] RST	

Example: A 10-year mortgage for $50,000 has a 14% annual
interest rate with monthly compounding. The loan has
constant principal payments. What is the amount of the principal payment and the amortization schedule for the first
three payments?

	Procedure	Press	Display
1.	Clear calculator and mode registers; select two decimal places.	ON/c 2nd **CLmode** 2nd **Fix 2**	0.00
2.	Press 2nd **Mode** until the "FIN" indicator is displayed.	2nd **Mode**	0.00
3.	Enter constant principal payment amortization program as listed on previous page.		0.00
4.	Reset program and clear mode register.	2nd **RST** 2nd **CLmode**	0.00
5.	Enter amount borrowed and divide by number of payments to determine constant principal payment and store as two decimal value.	50000 PV ÷ 120 = 416.67 PMT	416.67
6.	Enter annual interest rate and divide by number of payments per year and store.	14 ÷ 12 ÷ 100 = %i	0.01
7.	Compute first payments values.		
	a. Payment number.	R/S	1.00
	b. Interest.	R/S	583.33
	c. Total payment.	R/S	1000.00
	d. Balance.	R/S	49583.33

(continued)

(continued)

Procedure	Press	Display
Compute remaining payments using procedure in step seven.		
8. Second payment.		
a. Number.	R/S	2.00
b. Interest.	R/S	578.47
c. Total payment.	R/S	995.14
d. Balance.	R/S	49166.67
9. Third payment.		
a. Number.	R/S	3.00
b. Interest.	R/S	573.61
c. Total payment.	R/S	990.28
d. Balance.	R/S	48750.00

Wrap-Around Mortgages

When a lender loans the difference between the current value of a mortgaged asset and the underlying (old) mortgage balance, it is described as a wrap-around mortgage. Normally, the lender makes the payments on the original (underlying) mortgages and receives the payments on the new mortgage from the borrower.

Generally two types exist. First, an equal term situation where the wrap-around mortgage and the underlying mortgage have the same number of payments. Or second, an unequal term situation where the wrap-around mortgage and the underlying mortgage have a different number of payments. To solve for the yield of either type, draw a time-line diagram to determine the net cash flows for each payment period. The cash flows are entered, and the yield is computed. An example of each type is shown in the following examples.

Solving for the Lender's Yield—Equal Number of Payments

Kathy has a 10% mortgage with 180 remaining monthly payments of $746.50. The mortgage (underlying) has a current balance of $69,467.38. The mortgaged land and building have a current market value of $180,000.

She has applied for a $110,000 wrap-around mortgage from your firm. The new loan would have 180 payments of $1,464.92 at 14% annual with monthly compounding. What is the annual yield compounded monthly to your firm if the loan is made and the annual effective yield? (Note: Since payments occur at the end of each period, this is an ordinary annuity situation.)

First develop the time-line diagram shown below with all cash flows.

Wrap	+ 110,000.00	1464.92	1464.92
Less old mortgage	69,467.38	746.50	746.50
Net cash flows	40,532.62	718.42	718.42
	↓	↑ ···	↑
Payments	0	1	180

After determining the net cash flows, you are ready for the keystroke solution.

If the memory indicator does not display at least one data memory available, press [2nd] CP before entering the solution.

Procedure	Press	Display
1. Clear calculator and mode registers; select two decimal places.	[ON/c] [2nd] CLmode [2nd] Fix 2	0.00
2. Press [2nd] Mode until the "FIN" indicator is displayed.	[2nd] Mode	0.00
3. Enter number of payments.	180 [N]	180.00
4. Subtract old loan balance from wrap loan amount and enter as present value.	110000 [−] 69467.38 [=] [PV]	40532.62
5. Subtract old loan payment from wrap payment and enter.	1464.92 [−] 746.50 [=][PMT]	718.42
6. Compute annual yield with monthly compounding and store.	[CPT][%i][×] 12 [=][STO] 1	20.22
7. Compute annual effective yield.	12 [APR▸][RCL] 1 [=]	22.20

The annual nominal yield with monthly compounding is 20.22% which is equivalent to an annual effective rate of 22.20%.

Solving for the Lender's Yield—Unequal Number of Payments

Bob has a 9% mortgage on his ranch with a current balance of $345,850.48 and monthly payments of $3,111.71. He has 60 payments remaining with a balloon of $306,793.75 due along with the last $3,111.71 payment. His ranch is currently worth $1,500,000.

He has applied for a 13% wrap-around mortgage with your firm. He wants a loan of $750,000 which means he will receive ($750,000 – $345,850.48) $404,149.52. He also wants the payments computed on a 30-year term with the loan to be paid off at the end of 15 years. Thus, the payments are $8,296.50, and the balloon is $655,723.99. Assuming the wrap around has a 13% annual interest rate with monthly compounding, what is the annual yield with monthly compounding and the annual effective yield?

The first step is drawing the time diagram showing the net cash flows.

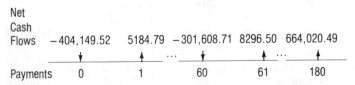

Wrap   655,723.99
Less   – 750,000.00   8296.50   8296.50 8296.50   8296.50
Old   345,850.48   – 3111.71   – 3111.71
Mortgage   – 306,793.50

Net
Cash
Flows   – 404,149.52   5184.79 – 301,608.71 8296.50 664,020.49

Payments   0   1   60   61   180

Your firm pays $404,149.52 to Bob. After netting the cash flows, the firm receives 59 payments of $5,184.79, pays out $301,608.71, receives 119 payments of $8,296.50, and a final payment of $664,020.49. (Note: Since payments vary, this is a variable/grouped cash flow situation.)

Procedure	Press	Display
1. Clear calculator and mode registers; select two decimal places.	ON/c 2nd CLmode 2nd Fix 2	0.00
2. Press 2nd **Mode** until the "CF" indicator is displayed.	2nd **Mode**	0.00
3. Enter cash flow at time zero as negative value.	404149.52 +/− PV	− 404149.52
4. Enter payment groups.		
a. First group.		
Amount.	5184.79	**5184.79**
Number.	2nd **Frq** 59	**Fr 059**
Store.	STO 1	**5184.79**
b. Second group.		
Amount.	301608.71 +/−	**− 301608.71**
Store.	STO 2	**− 301608.71**
c. Third group.		
Amount.	8296.50	**8296.50**
Number.	2nd **Frq** 119	**Fr 119**
Store.	STO 3	**8296.50**
d. Fourth group.	664020.49 STO 4	**664020.49**
5. Compute monthly yield.	CPT 2nd **IRR**	**1.2**
6. Enter payments per year and compute annual yield with monthly compounding.	X 12 = %i	**14.42**
7. Enter payments per year and compute annual effective rate.	12 APR► RCL %i =	**15.41**

The annual nominal yield is 14.42% which is equivalent to an annual effective rate of 15.41%.

The program shown below is used in the two examples
which follow. It allows you to prepare a mortgage amortization schedule for various mortgages where interest is
compounded. For a continuous printout, omit the four [R/S]
keystrokes.

The procedure for entering this program is shown in the
following example. Refer to the "Programming Keys" section
of chapter 1 for additional information on programming
procedures.

Mortgage Amortization Schedule

Step	Keystroke	Key Code	Step	Keystroke	Key Code
	[2nd] CP		15	[2nd] Bal	28
	[LRN]		16	[−]	75
00	[RCL]	71	17	[RCL]	71
01	[N]	21	18	[PV]	24
02	[SUM]	81	19	[=]	95
03	1	01	20	[+/−]	94
04	[RCL]	71	21	[2nd] Print	99
05	1	01	22	[R/S]	13
06	[2nd] Print	99	23	[RCL]	71
07	[R/S]	13	24	[N]	21
08	[RCL]	71	25	[2nd] Bal	28
09	[N]	21	26	[PV]	24
10	[2nd] Acc	27	27	[2nd] Print	99
11	[2nd] Print	99	28	[R/S]	13
12	[R/S]	13	29	[2nd] RST	37
13	[RCL]	71		[LRN]	
14	[N]	21		[2nd] RST	

Ordinary Mortgages

You have just sold a house, and the buyer wants an amortization schedule for the two months remaining in that year and for the annual interest and principal paid for the next year. The mortgage amount is $68,500 for 30 years with monthly payments of $771.15. The annual nominal interest rate is 13.25% with monthly compounding.

Procedure	Press	Display
1. Clear calculator, mode registers, and memories; select two decimal places.	[ON/c] [2nd] **CLmode** [2nd] **CLmem** [2nd] **Fix** 2	0.00
2. Press [2nd] **Mode** until the "FIN" indicator is displayed.	[2nd] **Mode**	0.00
3. Enter amortization program as listed on previous page.		0.00
4. Calculate and enter periodic interest rate.	13.25 [÷] 12 [=] [%i]	1.10
5. Enter payment amount.	771.15 [PMT]	771.15
6. Enter amount borrowed.	68500 [PV]	68500.00
7. Enter zero for future value and reset program.	0 [FV] [2nd] **RST**	0.00
Complete Monthly Schedule.		
8. Enter one for monthly payments.	1 [N]	1.00
9. Payment number.	[R/S]	1.00
10. Interest.	[R/S]	756.35
11. Principal.	[R/S]	14.80
12. Balance.	[R/S]	68485.20

(continued)

(continued)

Procedure	Press	Display
13. Repeat steps 9 through 12 for the second month.		
Payment number.	R/S	2.00
Interest.	R/S	756.19
Principal.	R/S	14.96
Balance.	R/S	68470.24

Compute amortization schedule for first whole year.

Procedure	Press	Display
14. Enter number of payments.	12 N	12.00
15. Repeat steps 9 through 12.		
Total payments.	R/S	14.00
Interest.	R/S	9060.87
Principal.	R/S	192.93
Balance.	R/S	68277.31

Note: To repeat a schedule, clear data memories and start at step eight since the program changes the value stored in the N register. Your calculator does not round to two decimal places when calculating principal, interest, or remaining balance. However, many lending institutions round to the nearest cent. For this reason, you may occasionally find a small difference between your calculations and their amortization schedules.

Graduated Payment Mortgages

The following example uses the program found at the beginning of the this section.

Sam's $40,000 mortgage has a 12.5% annual interest rate with monthly compounding. His payment schedule is:

Year	Payment Amount	Number of Payments
1	$359.11	12
2	377.06	12
3	395.92	12
4	415.71	12
5	436.50	12
6-30	458.32	300

He made 12 payments in 1981. What is the amount of interest charged for the first two payments in 1981 and the annual interest, principal, and remaining balance for the next three years?

Comment: GPM's normally have interest exceeding the monthly payment during the early years. This difference between interest and payment is shown as a negative number in the keystroke solution below and is added to the loan balance. The allowable amount deductable for a "cash basis" taxpayer is the actual interest paid; not accrued interest.

Procedure	Press	Display
1. Clear calculator, mode registers, and memories; select two decimal places.	[ON/c] [2nd] **CLmode** [2nd] **CLmem** [2nd] **Fix 2**	**0.00**
2. Press [2nd] **Mode** until the "FIN" indicator is displayed.	[2nd] **Mode**	**0.00**
3. Enter amortization program.		
4. Calculate and enter periodic interest rate.	12.5 [÷] 12 [=] [%i]	**1.04**

(continued)

(continued)

Procedure	Press	Display
5. Enter amount borrowed.	40000 PV	40000.00
6. Enter zero for future value and reset program.	0 FV 2nd RST	0.00
7. Enter amount of first year's payment.	359.11 PMT	359.11
8. Enter one for monthly payments.	1 N	1.00
9. Payment number.	R/S	1.00
10. Interest.	R/S	416.67
11. Principal.	R/S	−57.56
12. Balance.	R/S	40057.56
13. Repeat steps 9 through 12 for monthly amortization.		
Month two.		
a. Payment number.	R/S	2.00
b. Interest.	R/S	417.27
c. Principal.	R/S	−58.16
d. Balance.	R/S	40115.71
14. Compute values for remaining 10 payments in year one.		
a. Enter number of payments.	10 N	10.00
b. Total payments.	R/S	12.00
c. Interest for 10 payments.	R/S	4207.04
d. Principal for 10 payments.	R/S	−615.94
e. Balance.	R/S	40731.66
		(continued)

(continued)

Procedure	Press	Display
15. Compute values for year two.		
a. Enter number of payments.	12 [N]	12.00
b. Payment amount.	377.06 [PMT]	377.06
c. Total payments.	[R/S]	24.00
d. Annual interest.	[R/S]	5125.08
e. Annual principal.	[R/S]	−600.36
f. Balance.	[R/S]	41332.02
16. Year three.		
a. Payment amount.	395.92 [PMT]	395.92
b. Enter number of payments.	12 [N]	12.00
c. Total payments.	[R/S]	36.00
d. Annual interest.	[R/S]	5191.15
e. Annual principal.	[R/S]	−440.11
f. Balance.	[R/S]	41772.13
17. Year four.		
a. Payment amount.	415.71 [PMT]	415.71
b. Enter number of payments.	12 [N]	12.00
c. Total payments.	[R/S]	48.00
d. Annual interest.	[R/S]	5235.34
e. Annual principal.	[R/S]	−246.82
f. Balance.	[R/S]	42018.95

Note: Repeat step 17 for years 5 and 6, but do not change the payment amount after the sixth year.

Sam's loan balance has increased to $42,018.95 by the end of year four because the monthly payments do not cover the monthly interest. As a result, all of Sam's payments were for interest during the first four years.

6 REAL ESTATE

Real estate today is a dynamic field, with changes occurring almost daily. These changes are reflected in many aspects of financing, including mortgage packaging. Interested individuals range from the one-time investor who wants to know how much to invest in a single family house, to the builder/developer who is interested in tax benefits, depreciation allowances, and reduced taxable income.

In the past, the mathematical and statistical applications required for decision making were often tedious, time consuming, and prone to error. Today, however, many of the ratios, rates of return, and other analytical techniques that can help you arrive at the best real estate decision can be easily calculated. The range of the calculator's applications is limited only by your curiosity, imagination, and real estate knowledge.

The interest rate used in real estate calculations is normally an Annual Percentage Rate (APR) which is the same as an annual nominal rate. The APR may be converted to the interest rate per compounding period by dividing the APR by the number of compounding periods per year.

Comparing House Cost Per Square Foot

6 REAL ESTATE

You are looking at two houses. House A has 2,000 square feet of living space and costs $84,000. House B has 2,300 square feet of living space and costs $92,000. Based on cost per square foot, which house is the best buy?

Procedure	Press	Display
1. Clear calculator and select two decimal places.	ON/c 2nd **Fix** 2	**0.00**
2. Calculate cost per square foot of House A.	84000 ÷ 2000 =	**42.00**
3. Calculate cost per square foot of House B.	92000 ÷ 2300 =	**40.00**

House B costs $2 less per square foot than House A.

Calculation Of Down Payment

You plan to sell your house for an appraised value of $33,000. You still owe $27,500 on the mortgage. If the buyer wants to assume your mortgage, what percentage down payment would be necessary?

Procedure	Press	Display
1. Clear calculator and select two decimal places.	ON/c 2nd **Fix** 2	**0.00**
2. Calculate amount of down payment.	33000 ⊟ 27500 ⊜	**5500.00**
3. Calculate percentage of down payment.	⊡ 33000 ⊠ 100 ⊜	**16.67**

The buyer would have to make a 16.67% down payment.

Calculation Of
Agent's Commission

The total commission paid when selling a house is often 6% of the purchase price. The real estate firm gets half the total commission and the Listing Service gets the other half. Your agent earns half of the commission collected by the real estate firm. How much would your agent earn for selling your $38,000 home? What would the Listing Service get?

Procedure	Press	Display
1. Clear calculator and select two decimal places.	ON/c 2nd **Fix** 2	**0.00**
2. Calculate total commission.	38000 ✕ 6 % =	**2280.00**
3. Calculate amount of commission for real estate firm and Listing Service.	÷ 2 =	**1140.00**
4. Calculate amount of agent's fee.	÷ 2 =	**570.00**

The agent would earn $570 and the Listing Service would receive $1,140.00.

Average Yearly Appreciation Rate

The house you bought for $37,075 in 1972 was appraised at $74,000 in 1980. What was the average annual appreciation rate? If the rate of appreciation remains the same, what will the house be worth in three years?

Procedure	Press	Display
1. Clear calculator and mode registers; select two decimal places.	ON/c 2nd CLmode 2nd Fix 2	0.00
2. Press 2nd **Mode** until the "FIN" indicator is displayed.	2nd **Mode**	0.00
3. Enter number of years.	8 N	8.00
4. Enter original cost.	37075 PV	37075.00
5. Enter current market value.	74000 FV	74000.00
6. Compute annual appreciation rate.	CPT %i	9.02
7. Enter new period.	3 N	3.00
8. Enter new present value (current appraised value).	74000 PV	74000.00
9. Compute future value of the house after three years.	CPT FV	95893.28

The house is appreciating at an average annual rate of 9.02%. In three years, your house should be worth about $95,900 if the 9.02% appreciation rate continues.

You originally paid $60,000 for your house and now you want to sell it for a $25,000 profit. If the lending institution requires you to pay five points (5%), what is the selling price of the house?

If the memory indicator does not show at least one data memory available, press 2nd CP before entering the solution.

Procedure	Press	Display
1. Clear calculator and select two decimal places.	ON/c 2nd **Fix** 2	**0.00**
2. Press 2nd **Mode** until the "FIN" indicator is displayed.	2nd **Mode**	**0.00**
3. Enter one, subtract points, and store result.	1 ⊟ 5 % = STO 1	**0.95**
4. Add original price and profit.	60000 ⊞ 25000 ⊜	**85000.00**
5. Calculate selling price.	÷ RCL 1 ⊜	**89473.68**

To make a $25,000 profit and to meet the lending institutions requirements that five points be paid on the sale, you would need to sell your house for $89,473.68.

Home Improvement Loan (Long Term Versus Second Mortgages)

You have decided to buy a $64,500 house and would also like to make some improvements. You can finance the house for 30 years at an 11.25% annual interest rate, compounded monthly, with 10% down. You need $5,000 for improvements which you could borrow from another source. The improvement loan would be at 14% annual interest, compounded monthly, for two years. What would your monthly loan payment be for the two loans (during the first two years)?·What would your monthly loan payment be if the improvement loan were included in the original house loan (added to the purchase price of the house)?

If the memory indicator does not show at least one data memory available, press [2nd] **CP** before entering the solution.

Procedure	Press	Display
1. Clear calculator and mode registers; select two decimal places.	[ON/c] [2nd] **CLmode** [2nd] **Fix 2**	0.00
2. Press [2nd] **Mode** until the "FIN" indicator is displayed.	[2nd] **Mode**	0.00
A. Calculate the total monthly payment when the home and improvement loans are financed separately.		
3. Calculate and enter number of periods in home loan.	30 [X] 12 [=] [N]	360.00
4. Calculate and enter periodic interest rate.	11.25 [÷] 12 [=] [%i]	0.94
5. Calculate amount of home loan after down payment and enter as present value.	64500 [−] 10 [%] [=] [PV]	58050.00
6. Compute and store payment for home loan.	[CPT] [PMT] [STO] 1	563.82
7. Calculate and enter number of periods in home improvement loan.	2 [X] 12 [=] [N]	24.00

(continued)

6-7

(continued)

Procedure	Press	Display
8. Calculate and enter interest rate per month on home improvement loan.	14 ⌹ 12 ⌷ %i	1.17
9. Enter home improvement amount.	5000 PV	5000.00
10. Compute monthly payment for home improvement loan.	CPT PMT	240.06
11. Add home loan payment to calculate total payment for both loans if financed separately.	+ RCL 1 =	803.88

B. Calculate the total monthly payment for financing both loans for 30 years.

Procedure	Press	Display
12. Calculate and enter total number of payments.	30 X 12 = N	360.00
13. Calculate and enter periodic interest rate.	11.25 ⌹ 12 = %i	0.94
14. Calculate total amount for home and improvement loan.	64500 + 5000 =	69500.00
15. Subtract down payment and enter result as present value.	− 10 % = PV	62550.00
16. Compute total monthly payment.	CPT PMT	607.52

The combined loan payments would be $803.88 for the first two years. If the improvement loan could be included in the purchase price, the monthly payments would be $607.52 for 30 years.

Assume that a piece of property has 20 years remaining on a $22,000 per year lease, with payments made at the end of each year. The reversion value (FV) of the property is forecast to be $100,000. The applicable discount rate is 11% annual rate compounded annually. What should you expect to pay for the land today to meet the specified reversion value and discount rate?

This is a method used by appraisers when they forecast a constant income stream (ordinary annuity) and a reversion value (the value of the property at the end of the time period). It is natural to presuppose a "stabilized" level stream for discounting to the present value.

Procedure	Press	Display
1. Clear calculator and mode registers; select two decimal places.	[ON/c] [2nd] CLmode [2nd] Fix 2	0.00
2. Press [2nd] **Mode** until the "FIN" indicator is displayed.	[2nd] **Mode**	0.00
3. Enter number of payments remaining on lease.	20 [N]	20.00
4. Enter annual interest rate.	11 [%i]	11.00
5. Enter annual payment.	22000 [PMT]	22000.00
6. Enter reversion value.	100000 [FV]	100000.00
7. Compute present value of property.	[CPT] [PV]	187596.61

You should expect to pay $187,596.61 for the land.

REAL ESTATE

Buying Rental Property—Basic Example

One quick method that can be used to determine whether or not to buy a piece of rental property is to assume that you will buy only if the rental income from the property covers the taxes, maintenance, insurance, and loan payment for the value of the property. Assume that a house rents for $210 a month. You estimate that taxes, insurance, and maintenance will run $75 each month. If you can get a 25-year loan for the full cost of the house at 12.75% annual interest, compounded monthly, how much can you afford to pay for the house?

Procedure	Press	Display
1. Clear calculator and mode registers; select two decimal places.	ON/c 2nd **CLmode** 2nd **Fix** 2	0.00
2. Press 2nd **Mode** until the "FIN" indicator is displayed.	2nd **Mode**	0.00
3. Calculate and enter number of payments.	25 ✕ 12 = N	300.00
4. Calculate and enter periodic interest rate.	12.75 ÷ 12 = %i	1.06
5. Calculate and enter amount of rent applicable to loan payment.	210 − 75 = PMT	135.00
6. Compute loan amount necessary to fulfill your specifications.	CPT PV	12172.56

A $12,173 house would be within your purchase limit.

Investing in Rental Property—Complex Example

For investment purposes, you're considering buying a house that is presently rented for $375 per month (payable at the first of each month). You have $10,000 available cash for the investment. You realize that buying a house involves some risk, so you are planning the move only if you can make a sizable profit on the deal (15% annual rate compounded monthly).

After checking with a real estate agent, you find that you can buy the house by placing $10,000 down and assuming a $25,000 mortgage. You figure that your expenses, including mortgage payments, will be about $250 per month. You expect to keep the property for 10 years, sell the property, pay off the mortgage, and net $20,000. Ignoring taxes, should you invest in the house?

You are dealing with two types of cash flows: one, the income produced by the property (the monthly rental payments and the $20,000 profit from selling the house in ten years); and two, the expenses of buying the house (the monthly mortgage payment, taxes, insurance, maintenance, and down payment). To solve the problem, follow this procedure:

1. Find the present value of the income.
2. Find the present value of the expenses.
3. Compare the expenses to the income to see which is greater.

If the present value of the income equals or exceeds the present value of the expenses, you should buy the house.

REAL ESTATE

If the memory indicator does not show at least one data memory available, press [2nd] CP before entering the solution.

	Procedure	Press	Display
1.	Clear calculator and mode registers; select two decimal places.	[ON/c] [2nd] CLmode [2nd] Fix 2	0.00
2.	Press [2nd] **Mode** until the "FIN" indicator is displayed.	[2nd] **Mode**	0.00
3.	Calculate and enter desired monthly interest rate (use this as a discount factor in finding the present value).	15 [÷] 12 [=] [%i]	1.25
4.	Calculate present value of payments and sales price.		
	a. Calculate and enter number of regular rental payments.	10 [X] 12 [=] [N]	120.00
	b. Enter monthly rental income.	375 [PMT]	375.00
	c. Enter amount of gain on sale.	20000 [FV]	20000.00
	d. Compute and store present value of payments and gain (an annuity due situation since lease payments are usually made at the beginning of each period).	[2nd] **Due** [PV] [STO] 1	28038.40 (continued)

(continued)

Procedure	Press	Display
5. Compute present value of expenses.		
a. Enter zero for future value.	0 FV	**0.00**
b. Enter monthly expenses (mortgage payment, taxes, insurance, and compute present value of an ordinary annuity).	250 PMT CPT PV	**15495.71**
6. Add down payment to find total present value of expenses.	+ 10000 =	**25495.71**
7. Compare to present value of income.	+/− + RCL 1 =	**2542.69**

Purchasing the house will give you more than the 15%
annual return you want since the income will exceed the expenses by $2,542.69.

A lease that expires in 22 years requires a $15,500 monthly rental, payable in advance. As holder of this lease, you are negotiating with a prospective client who is considering offering $1,500,000 for the property holding. He wants to know what reversion value at the end of the 22-year lease period is necessary to realize a yield of 12% annual compounded monthly. A reversion value of $850,000 has been quoted to him. Do you agree or disagree?

The reversion value of the property is the difference between the future value of the monthly rentals and the future value of the offered sales price. The value entered for the present value in step six is negative so that it will be subtracted from the future value of the payments.

	Procedure	Press	Display
1.	Clear calculator and mode registers; select two decimal places.	ON/c 2nd CLmode 2nd Fix 2	0.00
2.	Press 2nd Mode until the "FIN" indicator is displayed.	2nd Mode	0.00
3.	Calculate and enter number of payments.	22 X 12 = N	264.00
4.	Calculate and enter periodic interest rate.	12 ÷ 12 = %i	1.00
5.	Enter rental payment as negative number since you are computing future value.	15500 +/− PMT	− 15500.00
6.	Enter lease sales price as a negative number.	1500000 +/− PV	− 1500000.0
7.	Compute future value of the difference between the lease payments and reversion value.	2nd Due FV	− 659592.23

The investor's advisors suggested a reversion value of $850,000, but your calculations indicate that the value of the property can drop to $660,000 at the end of 22 years and the investor will still receive his 12% return.

Assume that you are evaluating a property which will pro-
duce the following net operating income (cash revenues less
cash operating expenses), excluding mortgage payments or
depreciation deductions.

Year	1	2	3	4
Net Operating Income	$25,500	$29,000	$33,000	$36,000

The property will cost $200,000 with depreciable assets
worth $140,000. These assets have a depreciation life of 30
years, with no salvage value, and are depreciated by the
sum-of-the-years'-digits method.

To purchase the property, you need to invest $50,000 and
borrow an additional $150,000 for 30 years at an annual
interest rate of 14.5% compounded monthly. The monthly
payment is $1,836.83, and your tax rate is 48%.

For each of the next four years, project the net income
before tax, the tax liability, and the after-tax cash flow.

The annual depreciation expense values are computed as illustrated in "Sum-of-the-Years'-Digits" in Chapter 4, and the
annual interest paid on the mortgage is calculated as explained in Chapter 5. The calculated values are:

Year	1	2	3	4
Annual Depreciation Expense	9032.26	8731.18	8430.11	8129.03
Annual Interest Paid	21729.79	21681.40	21625.50	21560.93

After-tax Cash Flow Program

The program shown below is used for this example. While the example has annual cash flows, the program solves for after-tax cash flows on a monthly, quarterly, or annual basis. Just make sure that all items which include interest are consistent as to the time period, i.e., all items are monthly, quarterly, or annual. When using this program for a number of different applications, simply start at step four after the situation's cash flows are calculated.

The procedure for entering this program is shown in the following example. Refer to the "Programming Keys" section of chapter 1 for additional information on programming procedures.

Step	Keystroke	Key Code	Step	Keystroke	Key Code
	[2nd] CP		15	[%i]	22
	[LRN]		16	[=]	95
00	[PV]	24	17	[R/S]	13
01	[R/S]	13	18	[+/−]	94
02	[FV]	25	19	[+]	85
03	[R/S]	13	20	[RCL]	71
04	[+/−]	94	21	[PV]	24
05	[−]	75	22	[−]	75
06	[RCL]	71	23	[RCL]	71
07	[FV]	25	24	[PMT]	23
08	[+]	85	25	[=]	95
09	[RCL]	71	26	[R/S]	13
10	[PV]	24	27	[2nd] Print	99
11	[=]	95	28	[2nd] RST	37
12	[R/S]	13		[LRN]	
13	[×]	65		[2nd] RST	
14	[RCL]	71			

6

Projecting Income And After-Tax Cash Flows

Procedure	Press	Display
1. Clear calculator and mode registers; select two decimal places.	ON/c 2nd **CLmode** 2nd **Fix** 2	0.00
2. Press 2nd **Mode** until the "FIN" indicator is displayed.	2nd **Mode**	0.00
3. Enter after-tax cash flow program.		
4. Reset program to start.	2nd **RST**	0.00
5. Calculate and store annual mortgage payments.	1836.83 X 12 = PMT	22041.96
6. Enter tax rate as a percentage.	48 % %i	0.48
7. Enter net operating income before depreciation and interest payments for year one.	25500 R/S	25500.00
8. Enter annual depreciation expense.	9032.26 R/S	9032.26
9. Enter annual interest paid.	21729.79	21729.79
10. Calculate net income before tax.	R/S	– 5262.05
11. Calculate tax.	R/S	– 2525.78
12. Calculate cash flow after tax.	R/S	5983.82

(continued)

(continued)

Procedure	Press	Display

For subsequent years repeat steps 7, 8, 9, 10 and 11.

13. Year two.

	Procedure	Press	Display
a.	Net operating income.	29000 [R/S]	**29000.00**
b.	Annual depreciation.	8731.18 [R/S]	**8731.18**
c.	Annual interest paid.	21681.40	**21681.40**
d.	Net income before tax.	[R/S]	**−1412.58**
e.	Tax.	[R/S]	**−678.04**
f.	Cash flow after tax.	[R/S]	**7636.08**

14. Year three.

	Procedure	Press	Display
a.	Net operating income.	33000 [R/S]	**33000.00**
b.	Annual depreciation.	8430.11 [R/S]	**8430.11**
c.	Annual interest paid.	21625.50	**21625.50**
d.	Net income before tax.	[R/S]	**2944.39**
e.	Tax.	[R/S]	**1413.31**
f.	Cash flow after tax.	[R/S]	**9544.73**

15. Year four.

	Procedure	Press	Display
a.	Net operating income.	36000 [R/S]	**36000.00**
b.	Annual depreciation.	8129.03 [R/S]	**8129.03**
c.	Annual interest paid.	21560.93	**21560.93**
d.	Net income before tax.	[R/S]	**6310.04**
e.	Tax.	[R/S]	**3028.82**
f.	Cash flow after tax.	[R/S]	**10929.22**

Reference: Hoagland, Stone, and Brueggeman, *Real Estate Finance,* Chapter 11.

6 Projecting Income And After-Tax Cash Flows

Determining Net Present Value and IRR

After calculating the after-tax cash flows as described in the preceding example, finding the net present value and IRR is a simple procedure. This example is the same as the preceding one except that after-tax cash flows are known.

Example: You are evaluating a property that will cost $200,000, but you will only invest $50,000. The remainder is mortgaged. You plan to hold the property for four years at which time it can be sold for $275,000. You expect to have $102,199 after paying taxes and paying off the mortgage. What is the internal rate of return on this property with monthly compounding and with annual effective compounding, and what is the net present value using a 15% annual effective rate?

The cash flows are:

Annual Operating Cash Flows	5983.82	7636.08	9544.73	10929.22
Sale of Property				102199.00

Procedure	Press	Display
1. Clear calculator and mode registers; select two decimal places.	ON/c 2nd **CLmode** 2nd **Fix 2**	0.00
2. Press 2nd **Mode** until the "CF" indicator is displayed.	2nd **Mode**	0.00
3. Enter cash flows.		
a. First year.	5983.82 STO 1	**5983.82**
b. Second year.	7636.08 STO 2	**7636.08**
c. Third year.	9544.73 STO 3	**9544.73**
d. Fourth year:		
Add operating flow to proceeds from sale to find total cash flow.	10929.22 + 102199 = STO 4	**113128.22**
4. Determine net present value.		
a. Enter discount rate.	15 %i	**15.00**
b. Enter initial outlay as a negative value.	50000 +/− PV	**−50000.00**
c. Compute net present value.	CPT 2nd **NPV**	**31934.54**
5. Compute annual IRR and store results.	CPT 2nd **IRR** %i	**32.25**

This project has a net present value of $31,934.54 using an annual discount rate of 15% and an annual IRR of 32.25%. Solving for the modified financial management rate of return is discussed in Chapter 11.

Real estate loans are occasionally made where the interest is paid on a periodic basis and principal payments are delayed for a specified period of time. The loan may be paid off after a period of years or may be amortized over a subsequent time period. Because these loans are often structured to fit a customer's needs, the two following examples are representative but not exhaustive. They will, however, provide a guide to determining the net present value and IRR for such projects.

Interest Only Loan—Basic Example

Your company is evaluating a land purchase that requires an $80,000 down payment and a $320,000 loan. The loan requires no principal payments for five years, but you will make annual interest payments of 8% for two years, 10% for the next two years, and 12% the final year. The land can be rented to a farmer who will pay you $4,000 at the end of each year. You expect to sell the land at the end of five years for $550,000. Assuming an annual discount rate of 10%, compute the net payment value and also compute the IRR with annual compounding.

Solving this type of problem requires identifying the net cash flows for each year.

The amount of
interest paid is:

Year 1 and 2	8% × 320,000 = $25,600
Year 3 and 4	10% × 320,000 = $32,000
Year 5	12% × 320,000 = $38,400

By drawing a time-line diagram, you can determine the annual net cash flows.

Down Payment	−80,000					
Interest		−25,600	−25,600	−32,000	−32,000	−38,400
Rent		+4,000	+4,000	+4,000	+4,000	+4,000
Payment of loan						−320,000
Sale of land						+550,000
Net cash flows	−80,000	−21,600	−21,600	−28,000	−28,000	+195,600
Years	0	1	2	3	4	5

The next step is computing NPV and IRR.

Procedure	Press	Display
1. Clear calculator and mode registers; select two decimal places.	ON/c 2nd **CLmode** 2nd **Fix** 2	0.00
2. Press 2nd **Mode** until the "CF" indicator is displayed.	2nd **Mode**	0.00
3. Enter cash flows.		
a. First year.	21600 +/− STO 1	−21600.00
b. Second year.	STO 2	−21600.00
c. Third year.	28000 +/− STO 3	−28000.00
d. Fourth year.	STO 4	−28000.00
e. Fifth year.	195600 STO 5	195600.00
4. Enter original cash outlay.	80000 +/− PV	−80000.00
5. Enter annual discount rate.	10 %i	10.00
6. Solve for net present value.	CPT 2nd **NPV**	−36196.58
7. Solve for IRR.	CPT 2nd **IRR**	2.48

This project has a negative NPV of $36,197 which means you will earn less than the required 10% return. The IRR is 2.48% and is well below the 10% discount rate. It probably would not be a good investment.

6

Projects With Interest Only Loan

Interest Only Loan—Complex Example

You are considering an investment in land costing $150,000. You will pay $15,000 down and borrow the remaining $135,000. You can make annual interest only payments and start amortizing the principal with the first payment in the fourth year. You expect the property to sell for $500,000 at the end of the eighth year. The interest only portion of the loan will be 10% and the loan starting in the fifth year will be amortized over 30 years at an annual rate of 14% compounded monthly with end of month payments.

What is the payment schedule, the net present value using a 15% annual rate discounted monthly, and the IRR with monthly compounding.

Solving this problem requires four steps. First, determine the cash payments for the interest only portion of the loan and for the monthly amortization. Second, determine the loan balance at the end of the decision period. Third, determine the net cash flows for each period and enter them in the calculator. Fourth, compute NPV and IRR.

The time-line diagram below shows monthly periods because that is the shortest payment period in the problem. As a result, a number of zero monthly payments are shown for the interest only portion of the loan. This is necessary because the calculator always assumes *one* payment interval; as a result, you always select the shortest.

Down Pmt.	−15,000							
Loan Payoff								−132,881.59
Sale of Land								500,000.00
Annual Pmt.			−13,500		−13,500			
Monthly Pmt.			. . .			−1599.58	−1599.88 −	1599.88
Net Cash Flows	−15,000 0 0	−13,5000 0 0		−13,500	−1599.58	−1599.58		365,518.53
Months	0	1 11	12	25 35	36	37	95	96
No. of Payments	1	11	1	11	1	59		1

	Procedure	Press	Display
1.	Clear calculator and mode registers; select two decimal places.	[ON/c] [2nd] CLmode [2nd] Fix 2	0.00
2.	Press [2nd] Mode until the "FIN" indicator is displayed.	[2nd] Mode	0.00
3.	Enter amount borrowed and annual interest only rate to determine annual interest payments.	135000 [PV] [X] 10 [%] [=]	13500.00
4.	Enter annual rate for amortizing loan.	14 [÷] 12 [=] [%i]	1.17
5.	Enter number of periods for amortization.	30 [X] 12 [=] [N]	360.00
6.	Compute monthly payment starting with year four.	[CPT] [PMT]	1599.58
7.	Press [2nd] Mode until the "CF" indicator is displayed.	[2nd] Mode	1599.58
8.	Enter cash flows.		
	a. Initial outlay.	15000 [+/-] [PV]	−15000.00
	b. First year's payments. Eleven periods with zero payments and one period with a cash flow.	0 [2nd] Frq 11 [STO] 1 13500 [+/-] [STO] 2	−13500.00
	c. Second year's payments.	0 [2nd] Frq 11 [STO] 3 13500 [+/-] [STO] 4	−13500.00
	d. Third year's payments.	0 [2nd] Frq 11 [STO] 5 13500 [+/-] [STO] 6	−13500.00

(continued)

REAL ESTATE

**Projects With
Interest Only Loan**

(continued)

Procedure	Press	Display
e. All remaining payments except final cash flow.	1599.58 [+/−] [2nd] **Frq** 59 [STO] 7	− 1599.58
f. Final cash flow (rounded to nearest dollar).	365519 [STO] 8	365519.00
9. Enter desired annual discount rate and calculate monthly rate.	15 [÷] 12 [=] [%i]	1.25
10. Compute net present value.	[CPT] [2nd] **NPV**	23125.07
11. Compute IRR per month.*	[CPT] [2nd] **IRR**	1.65
12. Multiply by number of payments per year to determine annual nominal rate.	[X] 12 [=]	19.79

This project has a net present value of $23,125 using a 15% discount rate and an IRR of 19.79% with monthly compounding.

*Calculation requires approximately 2½ minutes.

7 LEASES

LEASES 7

The profitability of a personal or business-related lease is affected by many factors including payment amount, required return rate, residual value, and alternate investment opportunities. Before actually entering into any lease agreement, all factors should be carefully evaluated. With your calculator, you can quickly explore various types of leasing arrangements and use the results to make more informed decisions. In this chapter, residual value is the amount for which the lessor can sell the asset or the amount the lessee will pay for the asset at the end of the lease.

This chapter includes the following examples:

- leases with and without residual values (value of an asset at the end of lease)
- leases with advance payments made with the first payment
- leases with variable payments instead of constant payments
- personal lease-or-buy decisions.

Leases

7 LEASES

Determining Payment Amount

The JQ Company is leasing a machine with a current market value of $130,000 to the RO Company for three years. At the end of this time, the machine's market value should be $90,000. Lease payments are to be made at the beginning of each quarter. If the JQ Company wants to earn an annual return rate of 25% compounded quarterly, how much should the quarterly payments be? (Note: Since payments occur at the beginning of each period, this is an annuity due situation.)

Note: If the residual value is greater than the present value, a misleading answer results when computing PMT.

Procedure	Press	Display
1. Clear calculator and mode registers; select two decimal places.	[ON/C] [2nd] **CLmode** [2nd] **Fix 2**	0.00
2. Press [2nd] **Mode** until the "FIN" indicator is displayed.	[2nd] **Mode**	0.00
3. Calculate and enter number of periodic payments.	3 [×] 4 [=] [N]	12.00
4. Calculate and enter periodic interest rate.	25 [÷] 4 [=] [%i]	6.25
5. Enter present value of asset.	130000 [PV]	130000.00
6. Enter residual value of asset.	90000 [FV]	90000.00
7. Compute amount of periodic payment.	[2nd] **Due** [PMT]	9846.30

For the JQ Company to earn an annual interest rate of 25% compounded quarterly, the RO Company must make quarterly payments of $9,846.30.

LEASES 7

Determining Interest Rate

You lease a $10,400 automobile for 36 months and pay
$303.54 at the beginning of each month. If the automobile
has an assumed residual value of $3,500, find the annual
interest rate, compounded monthly, and the annual effective
rate. (Note: Since payments occur at the beginning of each
period, this is an annuity due situation.)

If the memory indicator does not show at least one data
memory available, press [2nd] CP before entering the solution.

Procedure	Press	Display
1. Clear calculator and mode registers; select two decimal places.	[ON/c] [2nd] CLmode [2nd] Fix 2	0.00
2. Press [2nd] Mode until the "FIN" indicator is displayed.	[2nd] Mode	0.00
3. Enter number of payments.	36 [N]	36.00
4. Enter present value of asset.	10400 [PV]	10400.00
5. Enter periodic payment.	303.54 [PMT]	303.54
6. Enter residual value of asset.	3500 [FV]	3500.00
7. Compute periodic interest rate.	[2nd] Due [%i]	1.58
8. Multiply by number of payments per year to determine annual nominal interest rate and store results.	[X] 12 [=] [STO] 1	19.00
9. Enter the number of payments per year and compute the annual effective rate.	12 [APR►] [RCL] 1 [=]	20.75

The lessor is earning an annual nominal return compounded
monthly of 19% which is equivalent to a 20.75% annual
effective rate.

Determining Payment Amount

The Boxer Company is leasing a machine to the Framing
Company for four years. The machine has a current market
value of $100,000 and a $15,000 residual value. Boxer is ask-
ing Framing to make one regular payment and three advance
payments in addition to the first regular payment when the
lease is signed. If Boxer wants a return equal to an annual
interest rate of 18% compounded monthly, how much is
each monthly payment?

You can solve the problem using this method:
1. With a periodic payment of $1, compute the present
   value of the annuity due.
2. Add the number of advance payments. Divide the current market value by the previous result to calculate the
   payment amount.

If the memory indicator does not show at least two data
memories available, press [2nd] CP before entering the
solution.

Procedure	Press	Display
1. Clear calculator and mode registers; select two decimal places.	[ON/C] [2nd] **CLmode** [2nd] Fix 2	0.00
2. Press [2nd] **Mode** until the "FIN" indicator is displayed.	[2nd] **Mode**	0.00
3. Calculate and enter periodic interest rate.	18 [÷] 12 [=] [%i]	1.50
4. Enter *total* number of compounding periods.	4 [X] 12 [=] [N]	48.00
5. Enter residual value.	15000 [FV]	15000.00
6. Compute present value of residual and store.	[CPT] [PV] [STO] 1	7340.43
7. Enter total payments and subtract advance payments.	48 [—] 3 [=] [N]	45.00

(continued)

(continued)

Procedure	Press	Display
8. Enter zero for FV.	0 [FV]	0.00
9. Enter one for payment.	1 [PMT]	1.00
10. Compute present value.	[2nd] **Due** [PV]	33.04
11. Add number of advanced payments and store results.	[+] 3 [=] [STO] 2	36.04
12. Subtract present value of residual from current market value and divide by results in step 11 to find payment.	100000 [−] [RCL] 1 [÷] [RCL] 2 [=]	2570.98

The Framing Company should make monthly payments of
$2,570.98.

Reference: Greynolds, Aronofsky, and Frame, *Financial Analysis Using Calculators: Time Value of Money.*

Determining Present Value

The Fortune Company is trying to decide whether to lease or
buy a machine from the Two Star company. The lease agreement would require Fortune to make payments of $1,850 at
the beginning of each month for eight years, and to make
two advance payments in addition to the first regular payment to replace the last two regular payments. Two Star is
willing to sell the machine for a price equivalent to the present value of a lease which would earn 17% annual interest,
compounded monthly. How much should Two Star charge for
the machine? (Assume that the residual value is $8,000).

Procedure	Press	Display
1. Clear calculator and mode registers; select two decimal places.	[ON/c] [2nd] **CLmode** [2nd] **Fix** 2	0.00
2. Press [2nd] **Mode** until the "CF" indicator is displayed.	[2nd] **Mode**	0.00
3. Calculate and enter periodic interest rate.	17 [÷] 12 [=] [%i]	1.42
4. Calculate amount of advance payments and enter.	2 [×] 1850 [=] [PV]	3700.00
5. a. Enter amount of periodic payment.	1850	1850
b. Enter number of payments (less advance payments).	[2nd] **Frq** 94	Fr 094
c. Store.	[STO] 1	1850.00
6. a. Enter zero.	0	0
b. Enter number of advance payments.	[2nd] **Frq** 2	Fr 002
c. Store.	[STO] 2	0.00
7. Enter residual value.	8000 [STO] 3 *	8000.00
8. Compute present value of lease.	[2nd] **Due** [2nd] **NPV**	102914.35

*Residual value occurs at the end of the 96th month, not the beginning of the month.

Two Star should charge $102,914.35 to earn 17% annually compounded monthly.

Determining Interest Rate

The Flower Company is leasing a special purpose machine to the Seed Company for nine years, with payments of $14,000 due at the beginning of each quarter. In addition to the first payment, the Seed Company must make four advance payments to replace the last four regular payments. If the current value of the machine is $250,000 and the residual value is $30,000, what annual rate of return, compounded quarterly, is Flower earning as well as the annual effective rate?

	Procedure	Press	Display
1.	Clear calculator and mode registers; select two decimal places.	ON/c 2nd CLmode 2nd Fix 2	0.00
2.	Press 2nd Mode until the "CF" indicator is displayed.	2nd Mode	0.00
3.	Calculate amount of advance payment.	4 ☓ 14000 =	56000.00
4.	Subtract total amount of advanced payments from current asset value and enter as negative value.	– 250000 = PV	–194000.00
5. a.	Enter periodic payment amount.	14000	14000
b.	Enter number of payments less advance payments ((9 × 4) − 4).	2nd Frq 32	Fr 032
c.	Store.	STO 1	14000.00

(continued)

(continued)

Procedure	Press	Display
6. a. Enter zero.	0	**0**
b. Enter number of advanced payments.	[2nd] **Frq** 4	**Fr 004**
c. Store.	[STO] 2	**0.00**
7. Enter residual value.	30000 [STO] 3	**30000.00**
8. Compute quarterly rate of return.	[2nd] **Due** [2nd] **IRR**	**6.90**
9. Multiply by number of payments per year to determine annual nominal rate and store results.	[X] 4 [=] [%i]	**27.59**
10. Enter number of payments per year and compute annual effective rate.	4 [APR▸][RCL] [%i][=]	**30.58**

The Flower Company is earning an annual rate compounded quarterly of 27.59%, which is equivalent to an annual effective rate of 30.58%.

Computing Interest Rate Earned

Your company has purchased a machine for $26,850. You
plan to lease the machine for five years to the XY Company.
The lease payments are made at the beginning of each
month with the payment amounts changing annually as
shown below. The machine has a residual value of $15,000.
What is the annual nominal rate with monthly compounding
and the equivalent annual effective rate?

Year	1	2	3	4	5
Beginning of Monthly Payments	$400	$500	$575	$650	$ 700
Residual at end of 5 years					$15000

Procedure	Press	Display
1. Clear calculator and mode registers; select two decimal places.	ON/C 2nd **CLmode** 2nd **Fix 2**	0.00
2. Press 2nd **Mode** until the "CF" indicator is displayed.	2nd **Mode**	0.00
3. Enter asset cost as negative value.	26850 +/- PV	− 26850.00
4. Enter cash flows.		
a. Year one amount.	400	400
Number.	2nd **Frq** 12	Fr 012
Store.	STO 1	400.00
b. Year two amount.	500	500
Number.	2nd **Frq** 12	Fr 012
Store.	STO 2	500.00
c. Year three amount.	575	575
Number.	2nd **Frq** 12	Fr 012
Store.	STO 3	575.00

(continued)

(continued)

Procedure	Press	Display
d. Year four amount.	650	**650**
Number.	[2nd] **Frq** 12	**Fr 012**
Store.	[STO] 4	**650.00**
e. Year five amount.	700	**700**
Number.	[2nd] **Frq** 12	**Fr 012**
Store.	[STO] 5	**700.00**
5. Enter residual value at end of year five.	15000 [STO] 6	**15000.00**
6. Compute monthly interest rate. *	[2nd] **Due** [2nd] **IRR**	**1.59**
7. Enter number of payments per year and calculate annual rate with monthly compounding; store results.	[X] 12 [=] [%i]	**19.02**
8. Enter number of payments per year and compute annual effective rate.	12 [APR▸] [RCL] [%i] [=]	**20.77**

The annual nominal interest rate with monthly compounding
is 19.02% which is equivalent to a 20.77% annual effective
interest rate.

*Calculation requires approximately 2 minutes.

A Simple Lease-Or-Purchase Decision

The sale price of a car is $5,000. You can purchase the car by making a $1,000 down payment and financing the balance at 1% per month for three years (36 months) with monthly payments of $132.86. You figure that your maintenance costs will be $15 a month and that you can sell the car for $2,500 at the end of the three years. Alternatively, you can lease a similar car for three years at $115 a month with the leasing company taking care of maintenance. The lease payments would be due at the beginning of the month. If your bank currently pays 5% annual interest, compounded monthly, which alternative would save you money in the long run?

Purchase option

Market Value					−$2500.00
Down payment	+$1000				
Monthly payments		+$132.86	+$132.86	+$132.86	+$ 132.86
Maintenance costs		+ 15.00	+ 15.00	+ 15.00	+ 15.00
Net cash flows	$1000	$147.86	$147.86	$147.86	−$2352.14
Months	0	1	2	35	36

Lease Option

PV = ?

Payment	$115	$115	$115	$115	$115	
Month	0	1	2	3	35	36

Note that the lease has 36 payments.

The problem can be solved by comparing the present value of the lease option to the present value of the purchase option. The present value of the purchase option can be determined as follows:

1. Find the net cash flows you pay by purchasing the car as shown above in the diagram.
2. Compute the present value of the cash flows determined above using the CPT key.
3. Compute the present value of the lease payments using the 2nd Due key.
4. The smaller of the values in step three and four indicates the best alternative.

Procedure	Press	Display
1. Clear calculator and mode registers; select two decimal places.	ON/c 2nd CLmode 2nd Fix 2	0.00
2. Press 2nd Mode until the "CF" indicator is displayed.	2nd Mode	0.00
A. Purchase car.		
3. Calculate and enter periodic interest rate.	5 ÷ 12 = %i	0.42
4. Enter initial outlay.	1000 PV	1000.00
5. Enter number of equal cash flows.	147.86 2nd Frq 35 STO 1	147.86
6. Enter final period cash flow.	2352.14 +/− STO 2	−2352.14
7. Compute present value of costs of purchasing.	CPT 2nd NPV	3781.01
B. Lease Car.		
8. Clear present value and memories.	0 PV 2nd CLmem	0.00
9. Enter monthly lease payment.	115 2nd Frq 36 STO 1	115.00
10. Compute present value of lease.	2nd Due 2nd NPV	3853.04
11. Subtract present value of purchase option (step seven) to determine best alternative.	− 3781.01 =	72.03

Based on these calculations, it costs $72.03 more to lease the car. Since this is a rather small difference, you can go on to weigh other reasons in favor of one decision or the other.

8 LOANS

LOANS 8

Even the most conservative spenders occasionally need to borrow money for special purchases. When you borrow money, you pay the lending institution a fee for using their money (interest). The amount of interest you pay depends on the percentage rate of interest, the length of time you borrow the money, and the way the interest is calculated. This chapter will help you evaluate various loan situations to determine which are the most economical.

Basically, interest rates are stated as either nominal or effective. An effective rate is the rate actually earned or paid for the specified time period, often a year. The interest rate is often stated as an effective rate in Europe. Nominal rates are most commonly used in the United States and are expressed as an annual rate where the annual rate divided by the number of compounding periods per year equals the periodic nominal rate. The Annual Percentage Rate (APR) is essentially the same as the annual nominal rate. For example, with a 12% APR, compounded monthly, the monthly interest rate used for compounding is 12%/12, or 1% per month.

Some types of credit transactions exclude certain fees or discounts when determining the APR. When you are borrowing money, it's a good idea to find out what items, if any, are excluded from the APR calculation. If any fees are excluded, the annual nominal rate which you actually pay is higher than the APR. Also, when quoting an APR, lending institutions often round the rate to the nearest 1/8%. Therefore, if you enter the quoted rate in the calculations, your answer (such as the payment amount) may differ slightly from the amount calculated by the lender.

Note: The applications in this chapter assume that payments are made at the end of each payment period. Use your calculator to explore these sample problems and try these concepts on your personal financial situations. You may find that you are able to make better decisions and, hopefully, pay less for your money.

Amount Of Payment

LOANS

You are planning to purchase a new small desk and chair set which is sale priced at $525. You can finance your purchase at 20% APR, compounded monthly, for two years. How much is the monthly payment?

Procedure	Press	Display
1. Clear calculator and mode registers; select two decimal places.	ON/c 2nd CLmode 2nd Fix 2	0.00
2. Press 2nd Mode until the "FIN" indicator is displayed.	2nd Mode	0.00
3. Calculate and enter number of payments.	2 X 12 = N	24.00
4. Calculate and enter periodic interest rate.	20 ÷ 12 = %i	1.67
5. Enter loan amount.	525 PV	525.00
6. Compute payment.	CPT PMT	26.72

Your monthly payment will be $26.72.

LOANS 8

Amount To Borrow And Amount Of Down Payment

You need to buy a new car which sells for $5,100. You can afford a monthly payment of $125, and the finance company charges 13.51% APR, compounded monthly. What loan and down payment amounts are required for a 48-month loan?

	Procedure	Press	Display
1.	Clear calculator and mode registers; select two decimal places.	ON/c 2nd CLmode 2nd Fix 2	0.00
2.	Press 2nd Mode until the "FIN" indicator is displayed.	2nd Mode	0.00
3.	Enter number of payment periods.	48 N	48.00
4.	Calculate and enter periodic interest rate.	13.51 ÷ 12 = %i	1.13
5.	Enter amount of payment.	125 PMT	125.00
6.	Compute loan amount.	CPT PV	4615.73
7.	Calculate down payment.	+/− + 5100 =	484.27

To buy the car, you must make a $484.27 down payment and borrow $4,615.73.

You need to buy a new refrigerator which will cost $895, and you can afford a monthly payment of $50. The finance company charges 18% APR, compounded monthly. How would it affect the loan if you made a $300 down payment, rather than financing the entire purchase? In other words, what is the difference in interest paid?

If the memory indicator does not show at least one data memory available, press (2nd) **CP** before entering the solution.

Finding The Savings That Result From A Down Payment

Procedure	Press	Display
1. Clear calculator and mode registers; select two decimal places.	[ON/C] [2nd] **CLmode** [2nd] **Fix** 2	0.00
2. Press [2nd] **Mode** until the "FIN" indicator is displayed.	[2nd] **Mode**	0.00
A. Find the interest paid without a down payment.		
3. Calculate and enter periodic interest rate.	18 [÷] 12 [=] [%i]	1.50
4. Enter amount of payment.	50 [PMT]	50.00
5. Enter amount of purchase price.	895 [PV]	895.00
6. Compute number of payments needed to pay off loan.	[CPT] [N]	21.00
7. Compute amount of interest paid without a down payment and store.	[CPT] [2nd] **Acc** [STO] 1	154.99
B. Find interest paid with a down payment.		
8. Enter the down payment and calculate new loan amount.	[RCL] [PV] [-] 300 [=] [PV]	595.00
9. Compute number of payments needed to pay off loan.	[CPT] [N]	13.21
10. Compute total interest paid.	[CPT] [2nd] **Acc**	65.31
11. Compare this amount to total interest paid without a down payment.	[+/-] [+] [RCL] 1 [=]	89.68

Almost $90 in interest is saved by making the $300 down payment as well as reducing the number of payments.

Amount Of
Final Payment

 LOANS

Assume that you borrow $3,920 at a 15% APR, compounded monthly, with monthly payments of $175. How many payments will you make? How much is the final payment?

Procedure	Press	Display
1. Clear calculator and mode registers; select two decimal places.	ON/c 2nd CLmode 2nd Fix 2	0.00
2. Press 2nd Mode until the "FIN" indicator is displayed.	2nd Mode	0.00
3. Calculate and enter periodic interest rate.	15 ÷ 12 = %i	1.25
4. Enter amount of payment.	175 PMT	175.00
5. Enter loan amount.	3920 PV	3920.00
6. Compute number of payment periods.	CPT N	26.44
7. Enter whole number value from step six and calculate loan balance after last regular payment.	26 CPT 2nd Bal	77.05
8. Enter loan balance (step 7) as present value*.	PV	77.05
9. Enter one for number of periods.	1 N	1.00
10. Enter zero for payment.	0 PMT	0.00
11. Compute amount of final payment.	CPT FV	78.01

You will make a total of 27 payments of $175 and a final payment of $78.01

*Since the loan balance ($77.05) after payment 26 is less than the payment amount, you can find the amount of the final payment by computing the future value of the loan balance thereby including the last period of interest.

Total Amount Of Interest Paid

You borrow $4,400 from your credit union to buy a car. The credit union charges 12.5% APR, compounded monthly. You will repay the loan in 36 monthly payments. How much will it cost to borrow the $4,400? (In other words, find the accumulated interest based on 36 payments.)

	Procedure	Press	Display
1.	Clear calculator and mode registers; select two decimal places.	ON/c 2nd CLmode 2nd Fix 2	0.00
2.	Press 2nd Mode until the "FIN" indicator is displayed.	2nd Mode	0.00
3.	Enter number of payments.	36 N	36.00
4.	Calculate and enter periodic interest rate.	12.5 ÷ 12 = %i	1.04
5.	Enter loan amount as present value.	4400 PV	4400.00
6.	Compute periodic payment.	CPT PMT	147.20
7.	Enter number of payments and calculate interest paid over life of loan.	36 CPT 2nd Acc	899.05

You will pay the credit union $899.05 in interest over the life of the loan.

Comparing
Time Payments

 LOANS

A salesman tells you that he will sell you the latest vacuum cleaner for payments of only $15 a month for three years at 21% APR. A store has advertised the same vacuum cleaner for $325. Which is the better deal?

One way to evaluate the time payment purchase is to compute the present value of the series of payments at the interest rate quoted by the seller and compare that amount to the sale price of the item.

	Procedure	Press	Display
1.	Clear calculator and mode registers; select two decimal places.	ON/c 2nd CLmode 2nd Fix 2	0.00
2.	Press 2nd **Mode** until the "FIN" indicator is displayed.	2nd **Mode**	0.00
3.	Calculate and enter number of payments.	3 ✕ 12 ═ N	36.00
4.	Calculate and enter periodic interest rate.	21 ÷ 12 ═ %i	1.75
5.	Enter payment amount.	15 PMT	15.00
6.	Compute present value of payments.	CPT PV	398.14

Comparing the present value of $398.14 to the store's purchase price of $325 shows the salesman selling the machine at a higher price.

Solving For The APR

A pickup truck sells for $4,817. To purchase the truck, you must make a down payment of $150 and 48 monthly payments of $127. The dealer quoted you an APR of 13.77%. Verify this quote and solve for the annual effective rate.

If the memory indicator does not show at least one data memory available, press ⟨2nd⟩ CP before entering the solution.

Procedure	Press	Display
1. Clear calculator and mode registers; select two decimal places.	⟨ON/c⟩⟨2nd⟩ CLmode ⟨2nd⟩ Fix 2	0.00
2. Press ⟨2nd⟩ **Mode** until the "FIN" indicator is displayed.	⟨2nd⟩ **Mode**	0.00
3. Enter number of payments.	48 ⟨N⟩	48.00
4. Enter amount of payment.	127 ⟨PMT⟩	127.00
5. Calculate and enter loan amount.	4817 ⟨−⟩ 150 ⟨=⟩⟨PV⟩	4667.00
6. Compute interest rate per month.	⟨CPT⟩⟨%i⟩	1.15
7. Multiply by number of payments to determine APR; store results.	⟨×⟩ 12 ⟨=⟩⟨STO⟩ 1	13.77
8. Enter number of payments per year and compute annual effective rate.	12 ⟨APR▸⟩⟨RCL⟩ 1 ⟨=⟩	14.68

The dealer quoted you the correct APR. The equivalent annual effective rate is 14.68%.

Comparing APRs

8 LOANS

When APRs have the same number of compounding and pay-ment periods per year they can be compared without any adjustments. But, when the APRs have different terms they should be converted to a common base such as Annual Effective Interest. For example, assume you can borrow $10,000 from either of two banks. Bank A charges 12% annually with monthly compounding and payments. Bank B charges 12.05% annually with quarterly compounding and payments. Which bank is offering you the lower interest rate?

If the memory indicator does not show at least one data memory available, press [2nd] CP before entering the solution.

LOANS **8**

Comparing APRs

Procedure	Press	Display
1. Clear calculator and mode registers; select two decimal places.	ON/c 2nd **CLmode** 2nd **Fix 2**	**0.00**
2. Press 2nd **Mode** until the "FIN" indicator is displayed.	2nd **Mode**	**0.00**
A. Convert bank A's rate.		
3. Enter number of compounding periods per year.	12 APR▸	**12.00**
4. Enter bank A's APR.	12	**12**
5. Convert to annual effective rate and store.	= STO 1	**12.68**
B. Convert bank B's rate.		
6. Enter number of compounding periods per year.	4 APR▸	**4.00**
7. Enter bank B's APR.	12.05	**12.05**
8. Convert to annual effective rate.	=	**12.61**
9. Compare to bank A's annual effective rate.	− RCL 1 =	**− 0.08**

Bank B offers the lower annual effective interest rate, so you will save .08% interest even though bank B has a higher APR than bank A.

Changing Payment Terms And Earning The Same Amount Of Interest

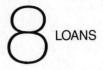

8 LOANS

Joe has arranged for a loan from his bank for $20,000 to be repaid over eight years. The bank quoted an APR of 14% with monthly payments and compounding, but Joe wants to make end of period quarterly payments. Assume the bank wants to earn the same annual effective rate on the loan under either set of payment terms. What are the payment terms? What are the payment amounts for monthly and quarterly payments?

Hint: In a situation as above, convert the original APR with monthly payments to an annual effective rate and then convert that rate to a nominal rate with quarterly payments.

If the memory indicator does not show at least one data memory available, press [2nd] CP before entering the solution.

Procedure	Press	Display
1. Clear calculator and mode registers; select two decimal places.	[ON/c][2nd] **CLmode** [2nd] **Fix** 2	**0.00**
2. Press [2nd] **Mode** until the "FIN" indicator is displayed.	[2nd] **Mode**	**0.00**
A. Evaluate monthly payment plan.		
3. Enter number of monthly payments.	8 [X] 12 [=][N]	**96.00**
4. Calculate APR per month.	14 [÷] 12 [=][%i]	**1.17**
5. Enter amount borrowed.	20000 [PV]	**20000.00**
6. Compute monthly payment.	[CPT][PMT]	**347.43**
B. Evaluate quarterly payment plan.		
7. Enter number of monthly payments and APR compounded monthly.	12 [APR▸] 14	**14**

(continued)

(continued)

Procedure	Press	Display
8. Convert to annual effective rate and enter.	$=$ STO 1	**14.93**
9. Enter number of payment periods per year for quarterly loan.	4 ◄EFF	**4.00**
10. Recall annual effective rate.	RCL 1	**14.93**
11. Convert to APR with quarterly payments.	$=$	**14.16**
12. Divide by number of payments per year and store results.	$÷$ 4 $=$ %i	**3.54**
13. Enter number of quarterly payments.	4 X 8 $=$ N	**32.00**
14. Compute quarterly payment.	CPT PMT	**1054.50**

The original monthly loan had an APR of 14% with monthly payments of $347.43. The quarterly loan, however, has an APR of 14.16% with quarterly compounding and quarterly payments of $1,054.50. Because both loan plans have the same annual effective rate of 14.93%, the rate of interest earned is the same, but the dollar amount paid is different.

Deferred Payments

8 LOANS

Determining Payment Amount

Julie has borrowed $5,000 to be repaid at the end of each month for 24 months with an APR of 13% compounded monthly. What is her monthly payment if she makes the first payment, (deferred one period) two months after the loan origination date?

Most loan payments are made at the end of the specified period (a month, in this case) and begin one period after the loan is made. Occasionally, however, the first loan payment might be deferred an additional period. If so, the monthly payment amount can be determined as follows.

1. Compute the future value of the original loan amount after one period.
2. Enter the future value as the present value and find the payment amount.

Note: This application assumes that compound interest is used for the deferred interest period.

Procedure	Press	Display
1. Clear calculator and mode registers; select two decimal places.	[ON/c] [2nd] **CLmode** [2nd] **Fix** 2	0.00
2. Press [2nd] **Mode** until the "FIN" indicator is displayed.	[2nd] **Mode**	0.00
3. Calculate and enter periodic interest rate.	13 [÷] 12 [=] [%i]	1.08
4. Enter amount borrowed.	5000 [PV]	5000.00
5. Enter number of periods until first payment. Subtract one and enter in N.	2 [−] 1 [=] [N]	1.00
6. Compute loan value at beginning of period when first payment is made.	[CPT] [FV]	5054.17
7. Enter loan value from step six or present value.	[PV]	5054.17
8. Enter zero.	0 [FV]	0.00
9. Enter number of payments.	24 [N]	24.00
10. Compute payment with deferred payments.	[CPT] [PMT]	240.28

If Julie defers her first payment for two months rather than the usual one month, her monthly payments will be $240.28.

Rule Of 78's

Amortizing a Loan

You are planning to borrow $2,500 at 11.5% APR, compounded monthly. You will make 24 monthly payments of $117.10 each. With the Rule of 78's method, prepare an amortization schedule for the first seven payments.

Loans amortized by the Rule of 78's method will reflect principal and interest amounts which differ from loans computed by the actuarial or compounded interest amortization method. The Rule of 78's method is similar to the sum-of-the-years'-digits depreciation method, except that you amortize the total interest on the loan.

The following program and keystroke solution generates an amortization schedule using the rule of 78's method.

The procedure for entering this program is shown in the following example. Refer to the "Programming Keys" section of chapter 1 for additional information on programming procedures.

Step	Keystroke	Key Code	Step	Keystroke	Key Code
	2nd CP		14	×	65
	LRN		15	RCL	71
00	RCL	71	16	PV	24
01	N	21	17	=	95
02	−	75	18	2nd Print	99
03	1	01	19	R/S	13
04	SUM	81	20	+/−	94
05	1	01	21	+	85
06	=	95	22	RCL	71
07	N	21	23	PMT	23
08	RCL	71	24	=	95
09	1	01	25	2nd Print	99
10	2nd Print	99	26	R/S	13
11	R/S	13	27	2nd RST	37
12	RCL	71		LRN	
13	N	21		2nd RST	

If you want the program to print on the printer without stopping, remove the three R/S keystrokes. But remember, you must stop the program when the loan is amortized or it will continue indefinitely.

If the memory indicator does not show at least one data memory available, press 2nd CP before entering the solution.

	Procedure	Press	Display
1.	Clear calculator and select two decimal places.	ON/c 2nd **Fix** 2	**0.00**
2.	Press 2nd **Mode** until the "FIN" indicator is displayed.	2nd **Mode**	**0.00**
3.	Enter Rule of 78's program.		
4.	Enter total number of payments; calculate and store sum of digits for number of payments.	24 STO 1 + 1 X RCL 1 ÷ 2 = FV	**300.00**
5.	Enter payment and amount borrowed and calculate interest on loan.	117.10 PMT X RCL 1 − 2500 =	**310.40**
6.	Divide by sum of digits and store results.	÷ RCL FV = PV	**1.03**
7.	Store total number of payments plus one. Enter zero and store. Reset program.	24 + 1 = N 0 STO 1 2nd **RST**	**0.00**
8.	Calculate interest portion of first payment.		
	a. Payment number.	R/S	**1.00**
	b. Interest.	R/S	**24.83**
	c. Principal.	R/S	**92.27**

(continued)

 LOANS

(continued)

Procedure	Press	Display
9. Calculate interest and principal portion of next six payments.		
a. Payment two.	R/S	2.00
	R/S	23.80
	R/S	93.30
b. Payment three.	R/S	3.00
	R/S	22.76
	R/S	94.34
c. Payment four.	R/S	4.00
	R/S	21.73
	R/S	95.37
d. Payment five.	R/S	5.00
	R/S	20.69
	R/S	96.41
e. Payment six.	R/S	6.00
	R/S	19.66
	R/S	97.44
f. Payment seven.	R/S	7.00
	R/S	18.62
	R/S	98.48

Note: You must stop the program when the loan is fully amortized or it will continue amortizing beyond the last payment date.

Finding the Payoff Amount

Use the same values as in the previous example and compare the procedures. You are planning to borrow $2,500 at 11.5% APR, compounded monthly. You will make 24 monthly payments of $117.10 each. By the Rule of 78's method*, find the rebate, the amount of interest paid, and the payoff amount after seven payments, without preparing an amortization schedule.

If the memory indicator does not show at least four data memories available, press [2nd] CP before entering the solution.

Procedure	Press	Display
1. Clear calculator and select two decimal places.	[ON/c][2nd] Fix 2	0.00
2. Press [2nd] Mode until the "FIN" indicator is displayed.	[2nd] Mode	0.00
3. Calculate total amount of interest on loan (number of payments × payment amount – loan amount) and store.	24 [STO] 1 [×] 117.10 [−] 2500 [=][STO] 2	310.40
4. Subtract number of last payment from total number of payments to calculate number of remaining payments.	[RCL] 1 [−] 7 [=][STO] 3	17.00
5. Calculate.	[+] 1 [×][RCL] 3 [=][STO] 3	306.00
	[RCL] 1 [+] 1 [×][RCL] 1 [=]	600.00
	[EXC] 3 [÷][RCL] 3 [=][STO] 3	0.51
6. Calculate rebate and store.	[RCL] 2 [×][RCL] 3 [=][STO] 4	158.30

(continued)

Rule Of 78's

8 LOANS

(continued)

Procedure	Press	Display
7. Calculate interest actually paid and store.	RCL 2 − RCL 4 = STO 4	**152.10**
8. Multiply number of payments made by payment amount and sum.	7 × 117.10 = +/− SUM 4	**− 819.70**
9. Enter loan amount and calculate payoff amount.	2500 + RCL 4 =	**1832.40**

The rebate is $158.30. You would pay $152.10 in interest. Immediately following the seventh payment, the payoff amount is $1,832.40.

*See Appendix A for the formula.

Reference: Greynolds, Aronofsky, and Frame, *Financial Analysis Using Calculators: Time Value of Money.*

LOANS

Amortizing Loans With Compound Interest

A company is buying a machine and will pay off the loan in six monthly installments. The machine costs $18,000, and the APR on the loan is 11.5%, compounded monthly. How much is the payment; what will the principal, interest, and remaining balance be after the third payment; and what is the complete amortization schedule?

Note: The program shown below is useful when preparing a complete amortization schedule.

The procedure for entering this program is shown in the following example. Refer to the "Programming Keys" section of chapter 1 for additional information on programming procedures.

Step	Keystroke	Key Code	Step	Keystroke	Key Code
	[2nd] CP		11	[x:y]	51
	[LRN]		12	[2nd] Print	99
00	1	01	13	[R/S]	13
01	[SUM]	81	14	[RCL]	71
02	1	01	15	1	01
03	[RCL]	71	16	[CPT]	12
04	1	01	17	[2nd] Bal	28
05	[2nd] Print	99	18	[2nd] Print	99
06	[R/S]	13	19	[R/S]	13
07	[CPT]	12	20	[2nd] RST	37
08	[2nd] P/I	26		[LRN]	
09	[2nd] Print	99		[2nd] RST	
10	[R/S]	13			

To have the program print without stopping, remove the four [R/S] keystrokes. But remember, you must press [R/S] to halt the program or it will continue indefinitely.

Amortizing Loans With Compound Interest

LOANS

	Procedure	Press	Display
1.	Clear calculator and mode registers; select two decimal places.	ON/c 2nd **CLmode** 2nd **Fix 2**	0.00
2.	Press 2nd **Mode** until the "FIN" indicator is displayed.	2nd **Mode**	0.00
3.	Enter Loan Amortization Program.		
4.	Enter APR and divide by number of payments per year.	11.5 ÷ 12 = %i	0.96
5.	Enter total number of payments.	6 N	6.00
6.	Enter amount borrowed.	18000 PV	18000.00
7.	Compute periodic payment.	CPT PMT	3101.42
8.	Enter payment amount rounded to nearest cent*.	3101.42 PMT	3101.42
	Individual payment amortization.		
9.	Enter third period and compute principal.	3 CPT 2nd P/I	2985.33
10.	Display interest.	x:y	116.09
11.	Enter third period and compute remaining balance.	3 CPT 2nd Bal	9128.77
	Amortization schedule using program.		
12.	Reset program and store zero.	2nd **RST** 0 STO 1	0.00
13.	Period number.	R/S	1.00
	Principal.	R/S	2928.92
	Interest.	R/S	172.50
	Remaining balance.	R/S	15071.08
			(continued)

(continued)

Procedure	Press	Display
14. Period two.	R/S	2.00
Principal.	R/S	2956.99
Interest.	R/S	144.43
Remaining balance.	R/S	12114.09
15. Period three.	R/S	3.00
Principal.	R/S	2985.33
Interest.	R/S	116.09
Remaining balance.	R/S	9128.77
16. Period four.	R/S	4.00
Principal.	R/S	3013.94
Interest.	R/S	87.48
Remaining balance.	R/S	6114.83
17. Period five.	R/S	5.00
Principal.	R/S	3042.82
Interest.	R/S	58.60
Remaining balance.	R/S	3072.01
18. Period six.	R/S	6.00
Principal.	R/S	3071.98
Interest.	R/S	29.44
Remaining balance.	R/S	0.03

The payment will be $3101.42. After the third payment, the principal will be $2985.33; the interest will be $116.09; and the remaining balance will be $9,128.77.

Since the payment amount entered in step 10 was rounded to two decimal places, you have a $0.03 remaining balance rather than a zero balance.

*Although the display in step six shows the payment amount rounded to two decimal places, the calculator uses all internal digits (up to 11) for subsequent calculations. For proper results, the payment amount must be rounded to two decimal places and then entered in step seven since payments must be in dollars and cents.

9 SAVINGS

SAVINGS 9

The amount of interest earned on a savings account is determined by several factors, including the annual interest rate and the compounding method. Banks or savings institutions can compound interest quarterly, weekly, daily, or continuously. With your calculator, you can quickly evaluate various interest rates and compounding methods to determine the best savings institutions for you.

When you are selecting a savings institution, keep in mind that, if the annual interest rates are equal, the account with the largest number of compounding periods per year will earn the most interest. You can evaluate unequal interest using your calculator to convert all rates to a common compounding method such as an annual effective interest rate. Also, savings institutions often quote the APR (annual percentage rate) rounded to the nearest 1/8%. As a result, using such a rounded rate can cause a difference between interest calculated by the institutions and your answer.

In this chapter, please remember that the value entered for [PMT] is negative so the calculator compounds the payments instead of discounting them. Also, the value entered for [N] is the total number of *compounding periods* for a single deposit. But, where a series of payments are made, the value for [N] is the total *number of payments*.

Regular Deposits

 SAVINGS

Finding the Amount of Regular Deposits Necessary to Have a Specified Amount in the Future

You want to deposit a constant amount of money in a savings account at the beginning of each month so that you will have $25,000 in ten years. How much should you deposit if the annual interest rate is 7% with monthly compounding, quarterly compounding, or continuous compounding?

If the memory indicator does not show at least two data memories available, press 2nd CP before entering the solution.

Procedure	Press	Display
1. Clear calculator and mode registers; select two decimal places.	ON/c 2nd CLmode 2nd Fix 2	0.00
2. Press 2nd **Mode** until the "FIN" indicator is displayed.	2nd **Mode**	0.00
A. Finding deposit amount with discrete compounding where number of compounding periods per year equals the number of deposits per year.		
3. Enter annual interest rate and divide by number of payments per year.	7 ÷ 12 = %i	0.58
4. Enter total number of deposits.	10 × 12 = N	120.00
5. Enter future value.	25000 FV	25000.00
6. Compute deposit amount with monthly compounding.	2nd Due PMT	– 143.60
B. Finding deposit amount when number of compounding periods per year are different from the number of deposits per year.		

(continued)

(continued)

Procedure	Press	Display
7. Enter number of compounding periods per year, annual interest rate, and compute annual effective rate. Store results.	4 [APR▸] 7 [=] [STO] 1	**7.19**
8. Enter number of deposits per year. Calculate interest rate per deposit period and enter.	12 [STO] 2 [◂EFF] [RCL] 1 [=] [÷] [RCL] 2 [=] [%i]	**0.58**
9. Calculate and enter number of deposits.	10 [X] 12 [=] [N]	**120.00**
10. Enter future value.	25000 [FV]	**25000.00**
11. Compute deposit amount with quarterly compounding.	[2nd] **Due** [PMT]	**−143.92**

C. Solving for deposit amount with continuous compounding.

Procedure	Press	Display
12. Enter annual continuous interest rate and divide by number of deposits per year.	7 [÷] 12 [=]	**0.58**
13. Convert continuous rate per month to equivalent discrete rate per month.	[%] [2nd] e^x [−] 1 [X] 100 [=] [%i]	**0.59**
14. Calculate and enter number of deposits.	10 [X] 12 [=] [N]	**120.00**
15. Enter future value.	25000 [FV]	**25000.00**
16. Compute deposit amount with continuous compounding.	[2nd] **Due** [PMT]	**−143.44**

You need to make deposits of $143.92 if the annual rate is compounded quarterly; $143.60 if the 7% annual interest rate is compounded monthly; and $143.44 if the annual rate is compounded continuously.

Regular Deposits

SAVINGS

Determining How Much Your Savings Will Be Worth

You plan to deposit $300 in a savings account at the begin-
ning of each month. How much will you have in the account
after four years if the annual interest rate is 6-1/4%
compounded monthly?

Procedure	Press	Display
1. Clear calculator and mode registers; select two decimal places.	ON/c 2nd CLmode 2nd Fix 2	0.00
2. Press 2nd Mode until the "FIN" indicator is displayed.	2nd Mode	0.00
3. Calculate and enter periodic interest rate.	6.25 ÷ 12 = %i	0.52
4. Enter amount of regular deposit as a negative value.	300 +/− PMT	− 300.00
5. Calculate and enter total number of deposits.	4 ✕ 12 = N	48.00
6. Compute future value with monthly compounding.	2nd Due FV	16396.85

You will have $16,396.85 in the account at the end of four
years.

SAVINGS

Applications With A Series Of Equal Deposits And A Beginning Balance

The following applications show you how to analyze situations where a series of equal deposits áre made and a beginning balance may exist. In the examples in this section, the value entered for N is the total number of equal payments and does not include the beginning balance, if any. Also, remember when you compound forward that the amount entered in PMT is a negative value.

Finding Future Value

You will have $5,000 in your savings account at the beginning of next month. At that time, you plan to start depositing $150 at the beginning of each month. How much money will you have in the account at the end of 22 months if the annual interest rate is 6.5% compounded monthly?

	Procedure	Press	Display
1.	Clear calculator and mode registers; select two decimal places.	[ON/c] [2nd] **CLmode** [2nd] **Fix 2**	0.00
2.	Press [2nd] **Mode** until the "FIN" indicator is displayed.	[2nd] **Mode**	0.00
3.	Calculate and enter periodic interest rate.	6.5 [÷] 12 [=] [%i]	0.54
4.	Enter number of regular deposits.	22 [N]	22.00
5.	Enter beginning balance of account.	5000 [PV]	5000.00
6.	Enter regular deposit as negative value.	150 [+/−] [PMT]	−150.00
7.	Compute future value with monthly compounding.	[2nd] **Due** [FV]	9144.55

After 22 months, you will have $9,144.55 with monthly compounding.

Applications With A Series Of Equal Deposits And A Beginning Balance

SAVINGS

Finding Payment Amount

Your savings account balance is $10,000 at the beginning of the month. You want to have $16,000 at the end of three years. How much should you deposit at the beginning of each month if the annual interest rate is 7.75% compounded monthly?

Procedure	Press	Display
1. Clear calculator and mode registers; select two decimal places.	ON/c 2nd CLmode 2nd Fix 2	0.00
2. Press 2nd Mode until the "FIN" indicator is displayed.	2nd Mode	0.00
3. Calculate and enter periodic interest rate.	7.75 ÷ 12 = %i	0.65
4. Enter number of regular deposits.	3 X 12 = N	36.00
5. Enter beginning balance of account.	10000 PV	10000.00
6. Enter future value of account.	16000 FV	16000.00
7. Compute regular deposit amount with weekly compounding.	2nd Due PMT	−83.45

With an annual interest rate of 7.75%, you need to make deposits of $83.45 with monthly compounding.

Often, a savings program will involve variable (uneven) deposits. The interest rate may change as well as the frequency of payments. You can compute the future value of such situations using your calculator and the short program in this section. How to compute the interest earned in such situations using the grouped cash flow keys is also shown.

Program to calculate Future Value of Variable Cash Flows.

The procedure for entering this program is shown in the following example. Refer to the "Programming Keys" section of chapter 1 for additional information on programming procedures.

Step	Keystroke	Key Code	Step	Keystroke	Key Code
	[2nd] CP		06	[2nd] Due	17
	[LRN]		07	[2nd] Bal	28
00	[2nd] Due	17	08	[PV]	24
01	[2nd] Bal	28	09	[2nd] Print	99
02	[PV]	24	10	[R/S]	13
03	0	00	11	[2nd] RST	37
04	[PMT]	23		[LRN]	
05	2	02		[2nd] RST	

Note: This program requires the number of deposit periods to be entered when deposits are omitted. The value calculated when [R/S] is pressed is the account balance one deposit period after the last deposit. To change the interest rate, simply enter the new value for [%i]. Interest rate changes are assumed to occur when the deposit is made. All deposits are assumed to occur at the beginning of a deposit period.

SAVINGS

Solving for the Future Value

If Jackie makes beginning of week deposits in an account
paying a 6.75% annual interest rate with daily compounding,
what is the balance in the account one week after the last
deposit? (Use a 365 day year.) The deposits are made as
follows:

Number of Weeks	Weekly Deposit
10	$ 20
4	0
30	40
25	50
1	100

The account had a balance of $300 when the first deposit
was made.

Procedure	Press	Display
1. Press [2nd] **Mode** until the "FIN" indicator is displayed.	[2nd] **Mode**	**0.00**
2. Enter program to calculate FV of variable cash flows.		
3. Clear calculator and reset program.	[2nd] **CLmode** [2nd] **Fix 2** [2nd] **RST**	**0.00**
4. a. Enter number of compounding periods per year and annual nominal interest rate. Store annual effective rate.	365 [APR▸] 6.75 [=] [STO] 1	**6.98**
b. Enter number of deposits per year and calculate annual nominal interest rate with weekly compounding.	52 [◂EFF] [RCL] 1 [=]	**6.75**

(continued)

(continued)

Procedure	Press	Display
c. Divide by number of deposits per year and enter.	⌹ 52 ⌹ %i	0.13
5. Enter beginning balance if any.	300 PV	300.00
6. Compute future value one period after last deposit in first group:		
a. Deposit amount as negative value.	20 +/− PMT	− 20.00
b. Number of deposits.	10	10.00
c. Compute future value at end of 10 weeks.	R/S	505.35
7. Future value one period after last deposit in second group. Since the deposits were skipped, enter a zero.	0 PMT 4 R/S	507.98
8. Third group.	40 +/− PMT 30 R/S	1752.62
9. Fourth group.	50 +/− PMT 25 R/S	3081.75
10. Last group.	100 +/− PMT 1 R/S	3185.88

One week after her last deposit, the balance is $3,185.88.

SAVINGS

Finding the Annual Interest Rate

Gabe recently withdrew all of the funds from his savings account one month after his last deposit. He withdrew $5,042.18. The account had a balance of $750 when the first deposit was made. His schedule of beginning of month deposits is:

Number of Monthly Deposits	Amount of Deposits
6	50
18	75
10	85
12	100

What is the annual interest rate he earned if compounding is monthly, annually, or continuous?

Procedure	Press	Display
1. Press 2nd **Mode** until the "CF" indicator is displayed.	2nd **Mode**	**0.00**
2. Clear calculator and fix decimal to two places.	2nd **CLmode** 2nd **Fix 2**	**0.00**
3. Enter initial balance of account if any as positive value.	750 PV	**750.00**
4. Enter first group of deposits.		
a. Amount.	50	**50**
b. Number.	2nd **Frq 6**	**Fr 006**
c. Store.	STO 1	**50.00**
5. Second group of deposits.	75 2nd **Frq 18**	**Fr 018**
	STO 2	**75.00**
6. Third group of deposits.	85 2nd **Frq 10**	**Fr 010**
	STO 3	**85.00**

(continued)

(continued)

Procedure	Press	Display
7. Fourth group.	100 2nd **Frq** 12	**Fr 012**
	STO 4	**100.00**
8. Enter final balance withdrawn one period after last deposit as a negative value.	5042.18 +/− STO 5	**−5042.18**
9. Compute monthly interest rate.*	2nd **Due** 2nd **IRR**	**0.48**
10. Multiply by number of deposits per year to determine annual nominal rate with monthly compounding.	X 12 = %i	**5.81**
11. Enter number of deposits per year and compute annual effective rate.	12 APR► RCL %i =	**5.96**
12. Compute annual continuous rate.	% + 1 = 2nd **lnx** X 100 =	**5.79**

The account had an average annual nominal rate of 5.81% with monthly compounding, with an equivalent annual effective rate of 5.96%, and an equivalent annual continuous rate of 5.79%.

Note: This procedure will not work if the payments have different periods.

*Calculation requires approximately 1½ minutes.

10 SECURITIES

SECURITIES 10

This chapter shows how your calculator can be used to help you evaluate investments in bonds, stocks, treasury bills, money market certificates, and certificates of deposit.

Included in this chapter are examples for finding return on stock with uneven dividends, with constant dividends, and an average return of non-dividend-paying stock. Also, the method for finding the theoretical value of stock is treated. Of great value to you as an investor is the section discussing treasury bills. Examples are given showing how to determine price and yield for treasury bills when either the yield or discount rate is known.

A simple method is given for determining the future value and yield for 6-month and 2-1/2 year money market certificates as well as the future value for certificates of deposit of less than $100,000. Finally, bonds with more than one coupon payment remaining are treated at length in this chapter.

Your calculator will compute prices and yields with great accuracy. The same calculation procedures practiced in the industry are used here in order to have solutions which agree with quoted figures. The approaches used in our programs to compute prices and yields are ones commonly used in the field. However, be aware that the examples shown are specific illustrations and do not take into account all of the factors that may affect the market. Historically, bond transactions have incorporated a variety of approximations, and many different types of calculations are still in use today. Because of this, the answers using the following methods may not agree exactly with the answers you get from all other sources.

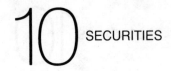
Stock Paying Uneven Dividends

Three years ago, you bought SPAD Airline stock for $65 per share. Upon receiving your final dividend, you sold the stock for $84.50. The quarterly dividends you received were:

Quarters	Amount	Number
1-4	.75	4
5-6	0	2
7	.25	1
8-11	.35	4
12	.20	1

Ignoring taxes, find the average annual return compounded quarterly and the equivalent annual effective rate.

Procedure	Press	Display
1. Clear calculator and mode registers; select two decimal places.	[ON/c] [2nd] **CLmode** [2nd] **Fix** 2	0.00
2. Press [2nd] **Mode** until the "CF" indicator is displayed.	[2nd] **Mode**	0.00
3. Enter the purchase price of the stock as a negative value.	65 [+/−] [PV]	− 65.00
4. Enter the first group of dividends.	.75 [2nd] **Frq** 4 [STO] 1	Fr 004 0.75
5. Enter second group.	0 [2nd] **Frq** 2 [STO] 2	0.00
6. Enter third group.	.25 [STO] 3	0.25
7. Enter fourth group.	.35 [2nd] **Frq** 4 [STO] 4	0.35
8. Add final dividend to sales price and enter.	.20 [+] 84.50 [=] [STO] 5	84.70
9. Compute the quarterly interest rate.*	[CPT] [2nd] **IRR**	2.79

(continued)

(continued)

Procedure	Press	Display
10. Enter number of payments per year and determine annual rate.	$\boxed{\times}$ 4 $\boxed{=}$ $\boxed{\%i}$	**11.14**
11. Enter number of payments per year and compute annual effective rate.	4 $\boxed{\text{APR}}$ $\boxed{\text{RCL}}$ $\boxed{\%i}$ $\boxed{=}$	**11.62**

The stock earns an annual rate of 11.14% with quarterly compounding or on annual effective rate of 11.62%.

*Calculation requires approximately 1 minute.

After-Tax Return Rate on a Stock Paying Constant Dividends

You have received a $0.50 dividend at the end of each quarter on the stock you bought five years ago for $20 per share plus a 1% commission per share. The stock is current-ly selling for $28 less a 1.25% commission. The tax rate on the dividends is 40% and the tax rate on the gain is 16%. If you sell the stock, what is your after-tax annual return rate with quarterly compounding and the equivalent annual effective rate?

If the memory indicator does not show at least one data memory available, press 2nd CP before entering the solution.

Procedure	Press	Display
1. Clear calculator and mode registers; select two decimal places.	ON/c 2nd CLmode 2nd Fix 2	0.00
2. Press 2nd **Mode** until the "FIN" indicator is displayed.	2nd **Mode**	0.00
3. Enter number of dividend payments.	5 ✕ 4 = N	20.00
4. Enter purchase price of stock, add commission, and enter results.	20 + 1 % = PV	20.20
5. Enter sales price of stock less commission.	28 − 1.25 % = FV	27.65
6. Calculate taxable gain.	− RCL PV =	7.45
7. Multiply by tax rate to find tax on gain.	✕ 16 % =	1.19
8. Subtract tax from net sales price to calculate after-tax cash flow from sale.	+/− + RCL FV = FV	26.46
9. Enter dividend amount and subtract tax to calculate after-tax dividend.	.50 − 40 % = PMT	0.30
10. Compute quarterly return.	CPT %i	2.68
11. Enter number of payments per year and calculate annual rate.	✕ 4 = STO 1	10.71
12. Enter number of payments per year and calculate annual effective rate.	4 APR► RCL 1 =	11.14

The annual return on the stock is 10.71% with quarterly compounding, which is equivalent to an annual effective rate of 11.14%.

Average Return Rate on a Non-Dividend-Paying Stock, Including Sales Commissions and Taxes

Three years and 45 days ago, you purchased some stock for $35 per share plus a 1-1/2% commission per share. You now have an opportunity to sell the stock for $48 a share less a 1.75% commission. The tax on the gain would be 17%. If you decide to sell, what is your after-tax annual yield?

Procedure	Press	Display
1. Clear calculator and mode registers; select two decimal places.	ON/c 2nd **CLmode** 2nd **Fix 2**	0.00
2. Press 2nd **Mode** until the "FIN" indicator is displayed.	2nd **Mode**	0.00
3. Calculate fractional years.	45 ÷ 365 + 3 = N	3.12
4. Enter sales price of stock, subtract commission, and enter.	48 − 1.75 % = FV	47.16
5. Enter purchase price of stock plus commission.	35 + 1.5 % = PV	35.53
6. Subtract net purchase price from net sales price to calculate taxable gain on sale.	RCL FV − RCL PV =	11.64
7. Multiply by tax rate to calculate tax liability.	X 17 % =	1.98
8. Subtract tax from net sales price to calculate after-tax cash flow from sale; enter result.	+/− + RCL FV = FV	45.18
9. Compute annual effective return.	CPT %i	8.00

Your after-tax annual return would be 8%.

Stock Paying Constant Dividends

You have an opportunity to buy a stock which pays a $0.65 dividend at the end of each quarter. The stock would probably sell for $180 at the end of four years. How much would you be willing to pay for the stock, disregarding taxes, if you want an annual return of 18% compounded quarterly and 18% compounded annually?

If the memory indicator does not show at least one data memory available, press [2nd] **CP** before entering the solution.

	Procedure	Press	Display
1.	Clear calculator and mode registers; select two decimal places.	[ON/c] [2nd] **CLmode** [2nd] **Fix 2**	0.00
2.	Press [2nd] **Mode** until the "FIN" indicator is displayed.	[2nd] **Mode**	0.00
3.	Enter quarterly interest rate.	18 [÷] 4 [=] [%i]	4.50
4.	Enter number of dividends paid.	4 [X] 4 [=] [N]	16.00
5.	Enter amount of dividend payment.	.65 [PMT]	0.65
6.	Enter future value of stock.	180 [FV]	180.00
7.	Compute theoretical stock price using quarterly compounding.	[CPT] [PV]	96.31

(continued)

(continued)

Procedure	Press	Display
8. Convert annual rate to equivalent rate per dividend period.		
a. Enter number of payments per year.	4 [STO] 1 [◄EFF]	**4.00**
b. Enter annual effective rate.	18	**18**
c. Calculate annual nominal rate with quarterly compounding.	[=]	**16.90**
d. Calculate interest rate per payment period and enter.	[÷] [RCL] 1 [=] [%i]	**4.22**
9. Compute theoretical price using annual compounding.	[CPT] [PV]	**100.29**

You could pay up to $96.31 per share to earn 18% annual compounded quarterly, or $100.29 per share to earn 18% compounded annually.

Treasury Bills

This section shows you how to compute the yield, price, or discount on Treasury Bills. The first examples show the procedures for bills maturing in less than six months while the latter examples cover bills maturing after six months. Actual calendar days are counted for the period until the bills are redeemed. If bills mature on a non-trading day, then you must add the necessary number of days to the days the bill is held. Also, when working from published discount and yield quotes, remember that most are calculated on the assumption that the actual trade occurs *two trading days after* the date of closing for the values quoted. Normally, you deduct two days if the closing date is a Monday, Tuesday, or Wednesday and four days if it is Thursday or Friday. In the Treasury Bill examples, actual dates and the number of days necessary for solution are given to illustrate the day counting procedure. All Treasury bill examples in this section use a price per $100, and the price and yield are based on the asked discount rate.

Finding the Price and Yield When Discount Rate is Known (Due in Less Than Six Months)

On Friday June 5, 1981, you place an order for $10,000 of Treasury bills due Thursday July 16, 1981. The asked discount rate is 16.43% as of closing on June 4. Assuming you actually purchased the bills on Monday June 8, what is the purchase price and the yield using industry practice and the annual effective interest rate? There are 42 days between 6/4/81 and 7/16/81, but allowing for two trading days and the weekend results in a 38 day holding period.

If the memory indicator does not show at least two data memories available, press (2nd) **CP** before entering the solution.

Procedure	Press	Display
1. Clear calculator and mode registers; select two decimal places.	[ON/c] [2nd] **CLmode** [2nd] **Fix** 2	0.00
2. Press [2nd] **Mode** until the "FIN" indicator is displayed.	[2nd] **Mode**	0.00
3. Enter number of days bills are held.	38 [STO] 1	38.00
4. Divide by number of days per year and enter.	[÷] 365 [=] [N]	0.10
5. Divide days held by 360 and multiply by the discount rate.	[RCL] 1 [÷] 360 [X] 16.43 [%] [STO] 2 [=]	0.02
6. Calculate price per $100 and store.	[+/−] [+] 1 [X] 100 [=] [PV]	98.27
7. Calculate dollar discount per $100.	100 [FV] [−] [RCL] [PV] [=]	1.73
8. Calculate yield using industry practice.	[RCL] 2 [X] [RCL] 1 [+/−] [+] 360 [=] [1/x] [X] 365 [X] [RCL] 2 [X] 100 [=]	16.95
9. Calculate annual effective interest rate.	[CPT] [%i]	18.30
10. Enter face amount purchased and calculate total purchase price.	10000 [X] [RCL] [PV] [÷] 100 [=]	9826.57

The price for $10,000 of treasury bills is $9,826.57 with a quoted industry yield of 16.95% and an annual effective rate of 18.30%. The industry rate is a simple interest rate without compounding which is the reason you should always calculate the annual effective rate.

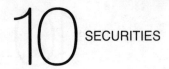

Finding the Price and Discount When the Yield is Known (Due in Less Than Six Months)

The yield for Treasury Bills maturing on Thursday November 5, 1981 as of closing on Tuesday June 2, 1981 is 15.66%. What is the Treasury Bill asked price per $100 and the percent discount based on the asked price? Assume the bills are actually purchased on Thursday June 4, 1981. There are 156 days between June 2, 1981 and November 5, 1981, but subtracting two trading days results in a 154 day holding period until maturity.

If the memory indicator does not show at least two data memories available, press (2nd) **CP** before entering the solution.

Procedure	Press	Display
1. Clear calculator and mode registers; select two decimal places.	⎡ON/c⎤ ⎡2nd⎤ **CLmode** ⎡2nd⎤ **Fix** 2	 **0.00**
2. Press ⎡2nd⎤ **Mode** until the "FIN" indicator is displayed.	⎡2nd⎤ **Mode**	**0.00**
3. Enter quoted yield as decimal.	15.66 ⎡%⎤⎡STO⎤ 2	**0.16**
4. Enter days until maturity.	154 ⎡STO⎤ 1	**154.00**
5. Calculate price per $100.	⎡×⎤⎡RCL⎤ 2 ⎡÷⎤ 365 ⎡+⎤ 1 ⎡=⎤ ⎡1/x⎤⎡×⎤ 100 ⎡=⎤⎡PV⎤	 **1.07** **93.80**
6. Calculate discount per $100.	⎡+/−⎤⎡+⎤ 100 ⎡FV⎤⎡=⎤	 **6.20**
7. Calculate discount rate.	⎡×⎤ 360 ⎡÷⎤ ⎡RCL⎤ 1 ⎡=⎤	 **14.49**
8. Full digits for price.	⎡RCL⎤ ⎡PV⎤ ⎡2nd⎤ **Fix** 9	 **93.802266**
9. Compute annual effective rate.	⎡2nd⎤ **Fix** 2 ⎡RCL⎤ 1 ⎡÷⎤ 365 ⎡=⎤ ⎡N⎤ ⎡CPT⎤⎡%i⎤	 **0.42** **16.37**

This bill sells for $93.80 per $100 with a discount of 14.49%. While the quoted yield is 15.66%, the annual effective interest rate is 16.37%.

Finding the Purchase Price When Yield is Given (Due in More Than Six Months)

The yield quoted at closing on Monday April 27, 1981 for treasury bills maturing on January 28, 1982 was 14.79%. Assume that you purchase $100,000 of these bills and the transactions occur two trading days later on April 29. There are 276 days between April 17, 1981 and January 28, 1982, but subtracting two trading days results in a 274 day holding period (days until maturity). What is the price, the discount rate and amount, and the annual effective rate?

If the memory indicator does not show at least three data memories available, press [2nd] **CP** before entering the solution.

Procedure	Press	Display
1. Clear calculator and mode registers; select two decimal places.	[ON/c] [2nd] **CLmode** [2nd] **Fix** 2	0.00
2. Press [2nd] **Mode** until the "FIN" indicator is displayed.	[2nd] **Mode**	0.00
3. Store quoted yield as decimal.	14.79 [%] [STO] 1	0.15
4. Enter days until maturity*.	274 [STO] 2	274.00
5. Calculate purchase price per $100.	[X] 2 [÷] 365 [−] 1 [X] [RCL] 1 [÷] 2 [+] 1 [=] [STO] 3	1.04
	[RCL] 1 [÷] 2 [+] 1 [X] [RCL] 3 [=]	1.11
	[1/x] [X] 100 [=] [PV]	89.79
6. Calculate discount in dollars.	[+/−] [+] 100 [FV] [=]	10.21
7. Calculate discount rate.	[X] 360 [÷] [RCL] 2 [=]	13.42
8. Calculate annual effective rate.	[RCL] 2 [÷] 365 [=] [N] [CPT] [%i]	15.43
9. Enter amount purchased and calculate total price.	100000 [X] [RCL] [PV] [÷] 100 [=]	89785.30

$100,000 worth of treasury bills will cost $89,785.30 with a discount rate of 13.42%. The annual quoted yield is 14.79% while the annual effective interest rate earned is 15.43%.

*If the number of days calculated in step four is less than 182 days, the solution procedures for Bills with less than six months to maturity should be used.

Finding The Yield And Price When Discount Rate is Given (Due in More Than Six Months)

Treasury Bills maturing on March 25, 1982 had an asked discount rate of 13.55% as of closing on Monday June 1, 1981. What is the quoted yield, annual effective rate, purchase price and dollar discount? Assume the bills are actually purchased on Wednesday June 3, 1981. There are 297 days between June 1, 1981 and March 25, 1982, but subtracting two trading days results in a 275 day holding period (days until maturity).

If the memory indicator does not show at least four data memories available, press [2nd] **CP** before entering the solution.

	Procedure	Press	Display
1.	Clear calculator and mode registers; select two decimal places.	[ON/c] [2nd] CLmode [2nd] Fix 2	0.00
2.	Press [2nd] **Mode** until the "FIN" indicator is displayed.	[2nd] **Mode**	0.00
3.	Enter days until maturity*.	295 [STO] 1	295.00
4.	Enter discount rate as a decimal.	[×] 13.55 [%] [=] [STO] 2	39.97
5.	Calculate price per $100.	[÷] 360 [+/−] [+] 1 [×] 100 [=] [PV]	88.90
6.	Calculate dollar discount.	[+/−] [+] 100 [FV] [=]	11.10
7.	Calculate and store.	[RCL] [PV] [%] [1/x] [+/−] [+] 1 [=] [STO] 3	− 0.12

(continued)

10 SECURITIES

(continued)

Procedure	Press	Display
8. Calculate and store.	2 [X] [RCL] 1	
	[÷] 365 [=]	
	[STO] 4	**1.62**
	[—] 1 [X] [RCL]	
	3 [X] 4 [+/−]	
	[+] [RCL] 4 [2nd]	
	x^2 [=] [√x̄]	
	[STO] 3	**1.71**
9. Calculate and store.	[RCL] 4 [+/−]	
	[SUM] 3	**−1.62**
10. Calculate industry yield.	[RCL] 4 [—] 1	
	[=] [1/x] [X] [RCL]	
	3 [X] 100 [=]	**15.02**
11. Calculate annual effective rate.	[RCL] 1 [÷] 365	
	[=] [N] [CPT] [%i]	**15.68**

The Treasury Bills have a quoted yield of 15.02% and an annual effective rate of 15.68%. The price per $100 is $88.90.

*If the number of days calculated in step three is less than 182 days, then use the procedure for bonds maturing in less than six months.

SECURITIES 10

**Investing In Money
Market Certificates
Of Deposit**

Individuals can invest in high yielding Money Market Certificates of Deposit, but certain conditions must be satisfied. Namely, minimum amounts are specified. Normally, a six month certificate requires a minimum investment and interest is not compounded during the period. Instead of compounding, a simple interest rate is applied as a ratio of days in the period. Many institutions, but not all, compute the daily rate using a 360 day year but the actual interest earned is computed using a 365 day year (366 in leap years). You should check the day count method employed by a savings institution before using the following applications.

Two and one-half year money market certificates, on the other hand, often compound interest daily and also require a minimum investment. The daily rate is determined by dividing the stated rate by 360 or 365 (366 in leap year). Again check on the exact method used when investing in money market certificates. Also, determine if interest is paid for the day of deposit and withdrawal so you can get an accurate day count.

Determining the Future Value and Yield on a Six Month Money Market Certificate

You invest $10,000 in a 14.741% six month money market certificate. Interest is not compounded, but is paid using a time factor of 182 days/360 days. This means the holding period is 182 days, and the daily interest earned per dollar is equal to .14741/360. What amount will you have after 182 days, and what is the annual effective interest rate (yield)?

If the memory indicator does not show at least one data memory available, press [2nd] CP before entering the solution.

Procedure	Press	Display
1. Clear calculator and mode registers; select two decimal places.	[ON/c] [2nd] CLmode [2nd] Fix 2	0.00
2. Press [2nd] **Mode** until the "FIN" indicator is displayed.	[2nd] **Mode**	0.00
3. Enter stated rate and calculate rate per day.	14.741 [÷] 360 [=]	0.04
4. Enter number of days and calculate fractional interest earned and store.	[×] 182 [=][STO] 1	7.45
5. Enter amount invested.	10000 [PV]	10000.00
6. Calculate interest.	[+][RCL] 1 [%]	745.24
7. Calculate total amount.	[=][FV]	10745.24
8. Divide days held by number of days in year and enter.	182 [÷] 365 [=][N]	0.50
9. Compute annual effective rate of return to six decimal places.	[CPT][%i] [2nd] Fix 6	15.51 15.505779

The certificate earns $745.24 in interest and has an annual effective yield of 15.51%.

Determining the Future Value and Yield on a 2-1/2 Year Money Market Certificate

You have just received a bequest of $5,000 from your uncle Sam. You have decided to invest in a 2-1/2 year money market certificate with a 12% stated rate. The interest rate per day is determined using a 360 day year, but is compounded daily using actual calendar days. This means you will have interest compounded for 912 days (365 [×] 2 [+] 182) assuming interest is not paid on the date of deposit.

What amount will you have after 2-1/2 years, and what is the annual effective yield?

Procedure	Press	Display
1. Clear calculator and mode registers; select two decimal places.	ON/c 2nd CLmode 2nd Fix 2	0.00
2. Press 2nd **Mode** until the "FIN" indicator is displayed.	2nd **Mode**	0.00
3. Enter stated annual rate and convert to 360 day compounding rate.	12 ÷ 360 = %i	0.03
4. Enter number of days until certificate matures.	365 × 2 + 182 = N	912.00
5. Enter amount invested.	5000 PV	5000.00
6. Compute future value.	CPT FV	6776.00
7. Enter number of days in year.	365 APR▸	365.00
8. Enter annual stated interest rate and compute annual effective rate.	12 =	12.75

The certificate will return $6,776.00 and earn an annual effective rate of 12.75%.

Finding the Yield and Future Value of Certificate of Deposit (Less Than $100,000)

You purchase a two year $3,000 certificate of deposit that has a 6.50% annual interest rate. The certificate states that interest is compounded daily based on a time factor of 365/360. This factor means that the daily rate is the stated rate divided by 360. What amount will you receive after two years, and what annual yield will you earn? (Use a 365 day year.)

If the memory indicator does not show at least two data memories available, press [2nd] CP before entering the solution.

Procedure	Press	Display
1. Clear calculator and mode registers; select two decimal places.	[ON/c] [2nd] **CLmode** [2nd] **Fix 2**	0.00
2. Press [2nd] **Mode** until the "FIN" indicator is displayed.	[2nd] **Mode**	0.00
3. Enter annual stated rate and convert to 365 daily interest rate.	6.5 [÷] 360 [=] [%i]	0.02
4. Enter amount invested.	3000 [PV]	3000.00
5. Enter number of days until maturity.	365 [X] 2 [=] [N]	730.00
6. Compute future value.	[CPT] [FV]	3422.62
7. Recall daily interest rate.	[RCL] [%i]	0.02
8. Enter 365 days and calculate annual nominal rate.	[X] 365 [STO] 1 [=] [STO] 2	6.59
9. Compute annual effective yield.	[RCL] 1 [APR▸] [RCL] 2 [=]	6.81

You will receive $3,422.62 at maturity, and the annual yield is 6.81%.

Bonds With More Than One Coupon Payment Remaining

A bond is a financial obligation made by a corporation or a government agency. The purchaser of a bond receives periodic interest payments, usually semi-annually, and receives the face value of the bond on the redemption date.

The interest payment each period is the interest rate printed on the bond divided by the number of payments per year and multiplied by the face value of the bond. For example, each six months a 14% $1000 bond with interest paid semi-annually would pay:

$$\frac{.14}{2} \times \$1000 = \$70$$

This semi-annual interest payment is also called the coupon payment. (The word coupon refers to the fact that the semi-annual payment is usually collected by presenting the company a printed coupon from a sheet that is part of the bond.) In this case, each coupon payment is $70, or 7%. This payment amount and the rate based on the face value of the bond remain constant. But bonds often sell at prices above or below the face value. A bond selling for an amount greater than the face (or par) value is said to be sold at a premium while a bond priced below par sells at a discount. The actual selling price can differ from the par value for many reasons. For example, a bond was originally sold when 10% was an acceptable return, but 13% is currently required in the market. Therefore, the bond would have to be sold below par (at a discount) to allow for the change in the return required in the market. This return required by the market is called yield.

More specifically, the yield is the return desired by the buyer. Because the face value of the bond and dollar amount of the coupon payment are fixed, the selling price, or present value, of the bond is adjusted to arrive at the yield. Thus, a bond sells at a premium when its coupon rate exceeds the market yield, while a bond sells at a discount if its coupon rate is below the market yield. The yield desired by an investor is a function of many factors including the issuer's bond rating, the state of the economy, and the amount of bonds purchased.

Bond prices are often quoted on a basis of 100% and
32nd's. Thus, a $1000 bond selling for $950 would be quoted
as 950. Bond prices quoted in 32nd's can be easily converted
to the dollar price as follows:

$$\text{dollar price} = \frac{\text{whole}}{\text{number}} + \frac{\text{number of 32nds}}{32}$$

So, a bond quoted as 98.14 where the 14 is 32nd's, has a
price per $100 of:

$$98 + \frac{14}{32} = \$98.4375$$

The dollar price is converted to a 32nd price as follows:

$$32\text{nd's} = \frac{\text{whole}}{\text{price}} + \frac{\text{decimal}}{\text{amount}} \times \frac{32}{100}$$

$$98 + .4375 \times \frac{32}{100} = \$98.14$$

Your calculator will accurately compute bond prices. The
following examples illustrate determining purchase price and
yield for bonds.

The approach included here for computing bond price and
bond yield is commonly used in practice. However, be aware
that the examples shown are specific illustrations and do
not take into account all of the factors that may affect the
bond market. Historically, bond transactions have incorporated a variety of approximations, and many different
types of calculations are still in use today. Because of this,
the answers from the following methods may not agree
exactly with answers you get from other sources.

References: Farish, et al, *Calculator Analysis for Business and Finance*, Chapter 5.
Greynolds, Aronofsky, and Frame, *Financial Analysis Using Calculators: Time Value of
Money*. Spence, Graudenz, and Lynch, *Standard Securities Calculation Methods*.

Bonds With More Than One Coupon Payment Remaining

Determining Purchase Price of a Bond Sold on an Interest Date

You're considering the purchase of a commercial bond as an investment. Suppose you want any bond that you purchase and hold to maturity to yield 7% interest compounded semi-annually. If the par value is $1000, how much should you pay for a 4% semi-annual bond which matures in six years?

Procedure	Press	Display
1. Clear calculator and mode registers; select two decimal places.	ON/c 2nd CLmode 2nd Fix 2	0.00
2. Press 2nd **Mode** until the "FIN" indicator is displayed.	2nd **Mode**	0.00
3. Calculate and enter yield per coupon period.	7 ÷ 2 = %i	3.50
4. Enter number of coupon payments.	6 × 2 = N	12.00
5. Enter redemption value of bond.	1000 FV	1000.00
6. Enter annual coupon rate and calculate amount of coupon payment.	4 % ÷ 2 × 1000 = PMT	20.00
7. Compute bond price.	CPT PV	855.05

The maximum purchase price of the bond is $855.05. Note that if you can buy the bond for less, your yield is higher. If you have to pay more, your yield is lower than your desired rate.

Finding Yield to Maturity on a Commercial Bond Purchased on an Interest Date

A 9% $1000 bond paying semi-annual interest has 13 remaining coupon payments. You can purchase the bond for $852.50 (ignoring commission). At this price, what is your yield to maturity and the annual effective rate?

If the memory indicator does not show at least two data memories available, press [2nd] CP before entering the solution.

Procedure	Press	Display
1. Clear calculator and mode registers; select two decimal places.	[ON/c] [2nd] **CLmode** [2nd] **Fix** 2	**0.00**
2. Press [2nd] **Mode** until the "FIN" indicator is displayed.	[2nd] **Mode**	**0.00**
3. Enter number of remaining coupon payments.	13 [N]	**13.00**
4. Enter redemption value of bond.	1000 [FV]	**1000.00**
5. Enter annual coupon rate and calculate amount of coupon payment.	9 [%] [÷] 2 [X] 1000 [=] [PMT]	**45.00**
6. Enter bond price.	852.50 [PV]	**852.50**
7. Compute semi-annual yield.	[CPT] [%i]	**6.18**
8. Multiply by number of payments per year to calculate yield to maturity with semi-annual compounding.	[X] 2 [STO] 1 [=] [STO] 2	**12.37**
9. Compute annual effective interest rate.	[RCL] 1 [APR▸] [RCL] 2 [=]	**12.75**

The annual yield to maturity with interest compounded semi-annually is 12.37%, and the equivalent annual effective interest rate is 12.75%.

Bonds With More Than One Coupon Payment Remaining

Determining the Yield to Maturity of a Bond Sold Between Interest Dates

A 12% $1,000 bond paying interest semi-annually is sold for $1,126.43. The bond has 21 remaining coupon payments. There are 184 days in the current coupon period and 74 accrued interest days. Compute the yield to maturity and the annual effective interest rate.

Your calculator will not solve directly for the yield, but the procedure shown below allows you to make a quick estimate and then to increase the accuracy of your initial estimate to the degree necessary.

If the memory indicator does not show at least four data memories available, press [2nd] CP before entering the solution.

	Procedure	Press	Display
1.	Clear calculator and mode registers; select two decimal places.	[ON/c] [2nd] CLmode [2nd] Fix 2	0.00
2.	Press [2nd] Mode until the "FIN" indicator is displayed.	[2nd] Mode	0.00
3.	Enter number of coupon payments, subtract one, and enter results.	21 [−] 1 [=] [STO] 1	20.00
4.	Store number of days in coupon period.	184 [STO] 2	184.00
5.	Enter and divide accrued interest days by coupon period days.	74 [÷] [RCL] 2 [=] [STO] 2	0.40
6.	Compute remaining days divided by coupon period days and sum.	[+/−] [+] 1 [=] [SUM] 1	0.60

(continued)

(continued)

Procedure	Press	Display
7. Enter number of coupon periods.	RCL 1 N	**20.60**
8. Enter redemption value and store.	1000 FV STO 3	**1000.00**
9. Enter annual coupon rate and calculate coupon payment.	12 % ÷ 2 X 1000 = PMT	**60.00**
10. Enter selling price and store.	1126.43 PV STO 4	**1126.43**
11. Calculate accrued interest and sum.	RCL PMT X RCL 2 = SUM 4	**24.13**
12. Calculate first rough estimate of yield to maturity.	CPT %i	**5.00**
13. Select number of decimals for accuracy.	2nd Fix 6	**5.002606**
14. Calculate improved estimate.		
a. Perform the following steps.	0 PV RCL 2 N CPT FV + RCL 4 = PV RCL 1 N RCL 3 FV	**1000.0000**
b. Calculate improved estimate.	CPT %i	**5.000054**

Repeat step 14 until the interest rate remains constant.

15. a.	0 PV RCL 2 N CPT FV + RCL 4 = PV RCL 1 N RCL 3 FV	**1000.0000**
b. Calculate improved estimate.	CPT %i	**5.000055**

(continued)

(continued)

Procedure	Press	Display
16. a.	0 [PV][RCL] 2	
	[N][CPT][FV][+]	
	[RCL] 4 [=][PV]	
	[RCL] 1 [N][RCL]	
	3 [FV]	1000.0000
b. Calculate improved estimate and stop because rate remains constant in 14b and 15b.	[CPT][%i]	5.000055
17. Multiply by number of coupon payments per year for annual yield to maturity.	[X] 2 [STO] 1	
	[=][STO] 2	10.000111
18. Compute annual effective rate.	[RCL] 1 [APR▸][RCL]	
	2 [=]	10.250116

The bond has a 10% yield to maturity with semi-annual compounding which is equivalent to a 10.25% annual effective rate.

Determining the Equivalent Tax-Free Yield on Taxable Bonds

You currently own a taxable bond that pays 10% dividends, and you are in a 38% income tax bracket. What dividend rate would you need to earn to get the same return?

Procedure	Press	Display
1. Clear calculator and select two decimal places.	[ON/c][2nd] **Fix** 2	0.00
2. Enter 100 and subtract income tax bracket percent.	100 [−] 38 [=][%]	0.62
3. Multiply by taxable yield to calculate equivalent tax-free yield.	[X] 10 [=]	6.20

You would need to earn a 6.2% annual dividend rate on a tax-free bond.

11 PRODUCTION MANAGEMENT

Sound production management is vital to the success of any business. Although the timing of managerial decisions is crucial, the mathematical calculations required to evaluate a situation can be lengthy and tedious to perform.

Here's where the real value of your calculator comes in. With a few simple keystrokes, you can easily explore many investment alternatives which may be crucial to your business. Your calculator can't tell you when to buy or sell a particular stock or assemble a "get rich quick" scheme for you, but you can use your calculator to evaluate investments and expenditures.

A company has annual requirements for 30,000 units with an $18 cost per purchase order placed. The cost of carrying one unit of inventory for a year is estimated to be $0.15. What is the Economic Order Quantity (EOQ); what are the minimum annual inventory costs; and how many times per year should inventory be ordered?

The EOQ is the quantity which should be ordered to minimize inventory costs during a specified time period, assuming no stock outs. Inventory costs consist of ordering costs plus carrying costs, and this model determines the EOQ and the minimum inventory costs for the time period. You can also find the number of times to order by dividing the number of units to be used during the time period by the EOQ. See Appendix A for the formula.

If the memory indicator does not show at least three data memories available, press 2nd CP before entering the solution.

**An Economic
Order Quantity
Inventory Model**

Procedure	Press	Display
1. Clear calculator, select two decimal places.	[ON/C] [2nd] **Fix** 2	**0.00**
2. Press [2nd] **Mode** until the "FIN" indicator is displayed.	[2nd] **Mode**	**0.00**
3. Enter cost per purchase order and multiply by number of units needed per period.	18 [X] 30000 [=]	**540000.00**
4. Multiply by two; store result.	[X] 2 [=] [STO] 1	**1080000.0**
5. Enter carrying cost per unit.	.15 [STO] 3	**0.15**
6. Calculate economic order quantity (EOQ).	[1/x] [X] [RCL] 1 [=] [√x] [STO] 2	**2683.28**
7. Calculate minimum inventory costs per period.	[RCL] 3 [X] [RCL] 1 [=] [√x]	**402.49**
8. Enter number of units required per period.	30000	**30000**
9. Divide by EOQ to calculate number of times to order per period.	[÷] [RCL] 2 [=]	**11.18**

The economic order quantity is about 2,683 units with a minimum annual inventory cost of $402.49. You would need to order about 11 times per year.

Determining How Much You Should Pay

You are considering the purchase of an annuity that pays $500 at the end of each month for the next 20 years. In addition to the final $500 payment, a lump sum amount of $5,000 will be paid. How much should you pay for the annuity if the annual interest rate is 9% compounded monthly?

Procedure	Press	Display
1. Clear calculator and mode registers; select two decimal places.	[ON/c] [2nd] **CLmode** [2nd] **Fix** 2	0.00
2. Press [2nd] **Mode** until the "FIN" indicator is displayed.	[2nd] **Mode**	0.00
3. Calculate and enter periodic interest rate.	9 [÷] 12 [=] [%i]	0.75
4. Calculate and enter number of payments.	20 [X] 12 [=] [N]	240.00
5. Enter amount of payment.	500 [PMT]	500.00
6. Enter amount paid in addition to final payment.	5000 [FV]	5000.00
7. Compute amount to pay (present value) for annuity.	[CPT] [PV]	56404.54

The value of the annuity is $56,404.54 with monthly compounding.

PRODUCTION
MANAGEMENT 11

Determining the Interest Rate

You have the opportunity to purchase a $50,000 annuity which will pay $570 at the end of each month for 10 years. A lump sum payment of $10,000 will be made in addition to the final monthly payment at the end of the annuity term. What is the annual interest rate with monthly compounding and annual compounding?

If the memory indicator does not show at least one data memory available, press [2nd] **CP** before entering the solution.

Procedure	Press	Display
1. Clear calculator and mode registers; select two decimal places.	[ON/c] [2nd] **CLmode** [2nd] **Fix 2**	0.00
2. Press [2nd] **Mode** until the "FIN" indicator is displayed.	[2nd] **Mode**	0.00
3. Calculate and enter number of regular payments.	10 [X] 12 [=] [N]	120.00
4. Enter amount of regular payment.	570 [PMT]	570.00
5. Enter amount invested.	50000 [PV]	50000.00
6. Enter lump sum amount received in addition to final payment.	10000 [FV]	10000.00
7. Compute monthly interest rate.	[CPT] [%i]	0.72
8. Multiply by number of payments per year and store.	[X] 12 [=] [STO] 1	8.61
9. Enter number of payments and calculate annual effective interest rate.	12 [APR▸] [RCL] 1 [=]	8.96

The annual interest rate is 8.61% with monthly compounding and 8.96% with annual compounding.

Determining the Present Value

You are evaluating a deferred annuity where the first monthly payment will be received at the end of 72 months. You will receive 36 payments of $500, 48 payments of $750, and 60 payments of $1,000. How much should you pay for the annuity if you can invest your money in other investments earning 12.5% annual compounded monthly?

Procedure	Press	Display
1. Clear calculator and mode registers; select two decimal places.	[ON/C] [2nd] **CLmode** [2nd] **Fix** 2	0.00
2. Press [2nd] **Mode** until the "CF" indicator is displayed.	[2nd] **Mode**	0.00
3. Calculate and enter periodic interest rate.	12.5 [÷] 12 [=] [%i]	1.04
4. Enter zero.	0	0
5. Enter number of deferred payment periods and store.	[2nd] **Frq** 72 [STO] 1	Fr 072 0.00
6. Enter deferred payments for first group.		
a. Amount.	500	500
b. Number.	[2nd] **Frq** 36 [STO] 2	500.00
7. Enter second group.		
a. Amount.	750	750
b. Number.	[2nd] **Frq** 48 [STO] 3	750.00
8. Enter third group.		
a. Amount.	1000	1000
b. Number.	[2nd] **Frq** 60 [STO] 4	1000.00
9. Compute price with monthly compounding.	[2nd] **Due** [2nd] **NPV**	25389.60

You should not pay more than $25,389.60 to earn 12% annual compounded monthly.

Determining the Interest Rate

A friend has offered to let you purchase an annuity for $60,000. The first payment will be made at the end of 90 months. You will then receive 24 payments of $2,000, 24 payments of $4000 and a final payment of $20,000. What is the annual interest rate assuming interest is compounded monthly, or annually?

Procedure	Press	Display
1. Clear calculator and mode registers; select two decimal places.	[ON/c] [2nd] CLmode [2nd] Fix 2	0.00
2. Press [2nd] **Mode** until the "CF" indicator is displayed.	[2nd] **Mode**	0.00
3. Enter cost of annuity as a negative value.	60000 [+/−] [PV]	− 60000.00
4. Enter zero.	0	0
5. Enter number of deferred payment periods and store.	[2nd] **Frq** 90 [STO] 1	Fr 090 0.00
6. Enter first group of defered payments.		
a. Amount.	2000	2000
b. Number.	[2nd] **Frq** 24 [STO] 2	2000.00
7. Enter second group.		
a. Amount.	4000	4000
b. Number.	[2nd] **Frq** 24 [STO] 3	4000.00
8. Enter final payment.	20000 [STO] 4	20000.00

(continued)

(continued)

Procedure	Press	Display
9. Compute interest rate per month.	[2nd] **Due** [2nd] **IRR**	**0.85**
10. Enter number of payments and calculate annual nominal interest rate. Store results.	[X] 12 [=] [%i]	**10.17**
11. Enter number of payments and calculate annual effective interest rate.	12 [APR▸] [RCL] [%i] [=]	**10.66**

This investment returns an annual interest rate of 10.17% with monthly compounding and 10.66% with annual compounding.

You can use a variety of time-value-of-money techniques to evaluate long term investments involving a series of cash flows. The techniques discussed here are Net Present Value (NPV), Internal Rate of Return (IRR), and Modified Financial Management Rate of Return.

NPV is the present value of a project's after-tax cash flows, less the outlay cash cost.

The IRR routine finds the interest rate which equates the present value of the cash flows with the outlay cost, assuming that the cash flows are reinvested at the IRR. If negative cash flows occur among a series of positive cash flows, you can get multiple IRR answers (which are usually invalid).

The Modified Financial Management Rate of Return method can be used instead of the IRR routine when multiple negative cash flows are present. This method assumes that the positive cash flows can be reinvested at your company's cost-of-capital rate. Any negative cash flows are discounted at a safe or sure interest rate, such as the rate on a savings account. Thus, the total present value of the negative cash flows represents the amount to be funded at the "safe" interest rate at the beginning of the project. The positive cash flows are compounded forward at the cost-of-capital rate to determine their future value. The Modified Financial Management Rate of Return is the interest rate which discounts the future value to an amount equal to the present value.

With your calculator, you can quickly apply these techniques to long term investment situations.

11 | PRODUCTION
MANAGEMENT

A Simple Example of Net Present Value and Rate of Return, Excluding Taxes

The Enterprise Paper Company is planning to pay $19,600 for a production machine which should save the company $5,000 a year for the next 10 years. The new machine will replace a current machine which has a zero market value. Enterprise requires a return rate of 20% on investments of this type. Excluding taxes and assuming a zero salvage value, find the net present value of the new machine, and the internal rate of return. (Assume that all cash flows occur at the end of each year.)

	Procedure	Press	Display
1.	Clear calculator and mode registers; select two decimal places.	ON/C 2nd CLmode 2nd Fix 2	0.00
2.	Press 2nd **Mode** until the "FIN" indicator is displayed.	2nd **Mode**	0.00
A.	Finding the net present value.		
3.	Enter number of payment periods.	10 N	10.00
4.	Calculate and enter periodic interest rate.	20 %i	20.00
5.	Enter amount of annual savings.	5000 PMT	5000.00
6.	Compute present value.	CPT PV	20962.36
7.	Subtract cost of machine to calculate net present value.	− 19600 =	1362.36
B.	Finding the internal rate of return.		
8.	Enter initial cash outlay.	19600 PV	19600.00
9.	Compute internal rate of return.	CPT %i	22.03

The net present value of the proposed purchase is $1,362.36. The internal rate of return is 22.03% assuming that the cash flows are reinvested at the same rate.

Finding the Modified Financial Management Rate of Return

A company is evaluating a $5,000 investment with a five-year life and after-tax cash flows of:

Year	1	2	3	4	5
Cash Flow	3500	− 2500	3800	− 3300	14500

The project has a net present value of $351.08 with a required 20% annual earnings rate. If the negative cash flows are funded by investing in a savings account which pays 5.5% compounded annually, what is the modified financial management rate of return?

The amount necessary to fund the negative cash flows is the sum of the present value of those cash flows.

The example can be represented on a time-line diagram:

	− $5000 Investment				FV = ?
Cash Flows		$3500 − $2500	$3800	− $3300	$14500
Year	0	1	2	3	4	5
Number of Compounding Periods (N) for Positive Cash Flows		4		2		0

Note: The procedure used for this solution assumes that the number of compounding periods per year equals the number of payment periods per year.

If the memory indicator does not show at least two data memories available, press [2nd] CP before entering the solution.

Procedure	Press	Display
1. Clear calculator and mode registers; select two decimal places.	[ON/C] [2nd] CLmode [2nd] Fix 2	0.00
2. Press [2nd] **Mode** until the "FIN" indicator is displayed.	[2nd] **Mode**	0.00
3. Enter "safe" interest rate.	5.5 [%i]	5.50
4. Enter period of first negative cash flow.	2 [N]	2.00
5. Enter amount of negative cash flow and store result.	2500 [FV]	2500.00
6. Compute present value of negative cash flow and store result.	[CPT] [PV] [STO] 1	2246.13
7. Repeat Steps 4-6 for each negative cash flow.		
a. Enter period of next negative cash flow.	4 [N]	4.00
b. Enter amount of negative cash flow.	3300 [FV]	3300.00
c. Compute present value of negative cash flow and add to memory.	[CPT] [PV] [SUM] 1	2663.82
8. Recall total present value of negative cash flows.	[RCL] 1	4909.95
9. Add initial cash outlay to calculate total present value and store.	[+] 5000 [=] [STO] 1	9909.95
10. Enter required interest rate.	20 [%i]	20.00

(continued)

(continued)

Procedure	Press	Display
11. Compute future value of positive cash flows.		
a. Period one.	4 N 3500	
	PV	3500.00
	CPT FV STO 2	7257.60
b. Period three.	2 N 3800	
	PV	3800.00
	CPT FV SUM 2	5472.00
c. Add period five cash flow.	14500 SUM 2	14500.00
12. Recall total future value of cash flows and enter as future value.	RCL 2 FV	27229.60
13. Enter number of periods (years).	5 N	5.00
14. Enter present value from step nine.	RCL 1 PV	9909.95
15. Compute the Modified Financial Management Rate of Return.	CPT %i	22.40

The Modified Financial Management Rate of Return is 22.40% which exceeds the required return rate of 20%.

Finding Net Present Value and IRR with Equal Cash Flows and Straight-Line Depreciation

Your company is considering the purchase of a $900,000 depreciable asset having a 10-year life. For depreciation purposes, the salvage value of the asset is $50,000, but your company expects to sell it for $75,000 at the end of 10 years. The annual cash inflows before taxes and depreciation total $385,000. The tax rate on the operating income is estimated at 40% and the tax rate on the gain when the asset is sold is 16%. If your company requires an 18% annual return rate compounded monthly on this investment, find the net present value of the asset and the IRR. (Assume that all cash flows occur at the end of each year.)

If the memory indicator does not show at least four data memories available, press [2nd] **CP** before entering the solution.

Procedure	Press	Display
1. Clear calculator and mode registers; select two decimal places.	[ON/c] [2nd] **CLmode** [2nd] **Fix 2**	0.00
2. Press [2nd] **Mode** until the "FIN" indicator is displayed.	[2nd] **Mode**	0.00
3. Convert annual return rate with monthly compounding to equivalent annual rate.		
a. Enter number of compounding periods per year.	12 [APR▸]	12.00
b. Enter annual rate compounded monthly.	18	18
c. Compute annual effective rate and enter results.	[=] [%i]	19.56
4. Enter number of cash flow periods.	10 [N]	10.00
5. Calculate capital gain taxable income (sale value – salvage value).	75000 [STO] 1 [−] 50000 [STO] 2 [=]	25000.00
6. Multiply by tax rate on gain to calculate amount of tax liability.	[×] 16 [%] [=]	4000.00
7. Subtract tax liability from future sales price to calculate after-tax cash flow from sale of asset.	[+/−] [+] [RCL] 1 [=] [FV]	71000.00

(continued)

Capital Budgeting

(continued)

Procedure	Press	Display
8. Calculate annual straight-line depreciation ((cost – salvage value) ÷ asset life)).	900000 [STO] 4 [−][RCL] 2 [÷] 10 [=]	85000.00
9. Calculate taxable income (annual cash flow before taxes – depreciation).	[+/−][+] 385000 [STO] 3 [=]	300000.00
10. Multiply by tax rate on income to calculate tax liability.	[×] 40 [%][=]	120000.00
11. Calculate after-tax cash flow before taxes minus tax liability.	[+/−][+][RCL] 3 [=]	265000.00
12. Enter after-tax cash flow as payment amount.	[PMT]	265000.00
13. Compute present value of cash flows and sale of asset.	[CPT][PV]	1139633.7
14. Subtract initial cash outlay to determine net present value.	[−][RCL] 4 [=]	239633.74
15. Enter initial cash outlay.	[RCL] 4 [PV]	900000.00
16. Compute internal rate of return with annual compounding.	[CPT][%i][STO] 1	26.93
17. Enter number of payments.	12 [◀EFF]	12.00
18. Compute annual rate with monthly compounding.	[RCL] 1 [=]	24.08

This investment has a net present value of $239,633.74. The return rate is 24.08% annual compounded monthly if the after-tax cash flows are reinvested at the IRR. The equivalent IRR with annual compounding is 26.93%.

11 PRODUCTION MANAGEMENT

Determining Net Present Value and Rate of Return with Variable Cash Flows and Accelerated Depreciation

You are evaluating an investment in a $60,000 depreciable asset with an eight-year life. The asset has a $10,000 salvage value for depreciation purposes but will probably sell for $4,000 at the end of eight years. The asset will be depreciated by the declining balance method with a factor of 200%. The operating cash flows before taxes and the depreciation for each year are:

Year	1	2	3	4	5	6	7	8
Operating Cash Flows	14000	22000	27000	34000	43000	39000	37000	30000
Depreciation*	15000	11250	8437.50	6328.13	4746.09	3559.57	678.71	0

With a tax rate of 45%, each cash flow is multiplied by 55% (100% – 45%) to determine the after-tax operating cash flows. The yearly depreciation is multiplied by 45% to obtain the tax benefit from depreciation. The results of these calculations are as shown below.

Year	1	2	3	4	5	6	7	8
After-tax Operating Cash Flows	7700.00	12100.00	14850.00	18700.00	23650.00	21450.00	20350.00	16500.00
Tax Benefit from Depreciation	6750.00	5062.00	3796.88	2847.66	2135.74	1601.81	305.42	0.00
Total	14450.00	17162.50	18646.88	21547.66	25785.74	23051.81	20655.42	16500.00

The tax rate on the gain or loss resulting from the sale of asset is 18%, and you require a return of 22% annually compounded annually on this project. What are the net present value and the internal rate of return?

*The model assumes that any operating losses will represent a tax savings on other taxable income.

Capital Budgeting

Procedure	Press	Display
1. Clear calculator and mode registers; select two decimal places.	[ON/C] [2nd] **CLmode** [2nd] **Fix** 2	**0.00**
2. Press [2nd] **Mode** until the "CF" indicator is displayed.	[2nd] **Mode**	**0.00**
3. Enter required return rate per period.	22 [%i]	**22.00**
4. Enter initial outlay as negative value.	60000 [+/−] [PV]	**− 60000.00**
5. Enter all but final after-tax cash flow.		
Period one.	14450.00 [STO] 1	**14450.00**
Period two.	17162.50 [STO] 2	**17162.50**
Period three.	18646.88 [STO] 3	**18646.88**
Period four.	21547.66 [STO] 4	**21547.66**
Period five.	25785.74 [STO] 5	**25784.74**
Period six.	23051.81 [STO] 6	**23051.81**
Period seven.	20655.42 [STO] 7	**20655.42**
6. Enter proceeds from sale of asset and subtract salvage value.	4000 [−] 10000 [=]	**− 6000.00**
7. Multiply by tax rate on sale of asset to calculate amount of tax.	[×] 18 [%] [=]	**− 1080.00**
8. Subtract tax liability from future sales price to calculate after-tax cash flow from sale of asset.	[+/−] [+] 4000 [=]	**5080.00**
9. Add final period after tax cash flow and store.	[+] 16500 [=] [STO] 8	**21580.00**
10. Compute net present value.	[CPT] [2nd] **NPV**	**9434.34** (continued)

(continued)

Procedure	Press	Display
11. Compute IRR with annual compounding. Store results.*	CPT 2nd IRR	26.87

The net present value of this investment is $9,434.34, and the IRR with annual compounding is 26.87%.

Investment Return Under Uncertainty

The estimated returns on certain projects must be based on assumptions about the economy. To estimate a return in this situation, probability factors can be assigned to the various conditions that could affect the value of the return. See Appendix A for the formula. Example: Your company is considering a project which will yield the following returns based on certain assumptions about the ecomony. The returns and the probability of each state of the economy are estimated as follows:

Future State of the Economy	Project Return as Percent	Probability of Economic State Occurring
Depression	− 10%	10%
Recession	− 1%	20%
Normal	8%	40%
Above Average	15%	20%
Boom	25%	10%

What is the expected value of the project and its standard deviation?

*Calculation requires approximately 2½ minutes.

Procedure	Press	Display
1. Clear calculator and mode registers; select two decimal places.	[ON/c] [2nd] **CLmode** [2nd] **Fix** 2	0.00
2. Press [2nd] **Mode** until the "STAT" indicator is displayed.	[2nd] **Mode**	0.00
3. Enter first project return percentage and probability of occurring as a percentage.	10 [+/−] [2nd] **Frq** 10 [Σ+]	10.00
4. Repeat step three for each set of data.		
a. Second estimated return.	1 [+/−] [2nd] **Frq** 20 [Σ+]	30.00
b. Third estimated return.	8 [2nd] **Frq** 40 [Σ+]	70.00
c. Fourth estimated return.	15 [2nd] **Frq** 20 [Σ+]	90.00
d. Fifth estimated return.	25 [2nd] **Frq** 10 [Σ+]	100.00
5. Compute expected value of project return.	[ȳ]	7.50
6. Compute standard deviation of expected value of return.	[σn]	9.33

The estimated return of the project is 7.5%, and its standard deviation is 9.33%.

Reference: Weston and Brigham, *Managerial Finance.*

12 STATISTICS

STATISTICS 12

Whether you need to analyze the volume of sales in a store, project overhead expenses, or forecast the possible effects of advertising on income, the statistics branch of mathematics can be an invaluable aid. However, performing the calculations can be a lengthy and time-consuming process. The statistical keys on your calculator will help you quickly perform the complex computations, leaving you with more time to analyze the results.

This chapter illustrates common business applications of statistics. Select the example which fits your needs, and then enter your values instead of those in the example.

There are basically two types of statistics. One is descriptive statistics, which involves collecting, grouping, and presenting large sets of data in ways that can be easily understood or assimilated. The other kind, inductive statistics or statistical inference, is used to draw conclusions from your observed data—to estimate population parameters from sample data, for example, and/or to predict trends and explore probabilities.

For problems involving descriptive statistics, several statistical calculations are used to "describe" the characteristics of the data set. One of the most common is finding the mean, or average, of the data. When you press $\boxed{\bar{x}}$, the calculator computes the mean of your data (the sum of the values divided by the number of values).

Standard deviation, or the "spread" (distribution) of your data points, is another frequently calculated descriptive statistic. Your calculator has two standard deviation keys, $\boxed{\sigma n}$ and $\boxed{\sigma n\text{-}1}$. $\boxed{\sigma n}$ is used to calculate the standard deviation of a population (a complete data set). Pressing $\boxed{\sigma n\text{-}1}$ calculates an estimated standard deviation based on a sample (a set of elements selected randomly to represent a population).

The difference between the two keys is the weighting given by the n factor used in the calculations (n is the number of elements in the population or sample). When your data set represents a whole population, press ⌐On⌐ to calculate the standard deviation using n weighting (dividing by the number of elements in the population). With sample data, press ⌐On-1⌐ to estimate the standard deviation of the whole population with n − 1 weighting (dividing by the number of elements in the sample minus one).

Note: The difference between the estimated standard deviation (based on a sample) and the population standard deviation becomes very small for over 30 sample data points.

Linear Regression

One of the inferential statistical procedures illustrated in this chapter is linear regression. In linear regression, you usually have data expressed as pairs of variables (x,y) that you could plot on a graph. The calculator mathematically draws a straight-line graph through the set of data points. The actual placement of the line is determined by a least squares linear regression that minimizes the sum of the squares of the deviation of the y values from the straight line of best fit. The equation is in the form

$$y = ax + b$$

where a is the slope of the line and b is the y-intercept (where the line crosses the y-axis).

In most instances, the x variable is considered the independent variable, while y is the dependent variable. The relationship between the two sets of variables (x and y), as defined by the equation, can be used to find the slope, y-intercept, correlation coefficient, and index of determination. The correlation coefficient ([2nd] **Corr**) tells you the strength of the linear relationship. The closer to $+1$ or -1 the value, the stronger the linear relationship. The index of determination ([2nd] **Corr** [2nd] x^2) tells you how well the line "fits" the data. The closer the value is to ± 1, the better the fit.

For trend line analysis, your calculator automatically adds 1 to the x variable for you. This means that you can enter the first x value and press [x:y], then enter the y value and press [Σ+]. Then you can enter the second data set by just entering the y value and pressing [Σ+]. The calculator automatically increments the x variable for you by one for each entry. This comes in handy when you're analyzing data from successive years.

Note: It is not statistically valid to compute an x (independent) value on the basis of a y (dependent) value or to compute a y value on the basis of an x which is outside the range of entered x values. However, trend line analysis and forecasting calculations often use these computations to make predictions or estimations of probability about the future. When you perform such calculations, it's important to remember that the actual values may differ from the calculated values, which only indicate what could happen based on the data you've entered.

Sample

Your store has just received a large shipment of candy with each box containing 16 ounces. You decide to weigh 30 boxes of candy. What is the mean, standard deviation and variance of the sample?

Number of Boxes	Weight in Ounces
1	15.
5	15.4
10	15.8
12	16.01
1	16.70
1	17.

STATISTICS **12**

**Mean And
Standard Deviation**

Procedure	Press	Display
1. Clear calculator and mode registers; select two decimal places.	[ON/c] [2nd] **CLmode** [2nd] **Fix 2**	0.00
2. Press [2nd] **Mode** until the "STAT" indicator is displayed.	[2nd] **Mode**	0.00
3. Enter data (calculator displays current number of data entries).		
a. Enter first weight group.	15 [Σ+]	1.00
b. Enter second group:		
Weight.	15.4	15.4
Number.	[2nd] **Frq** 5	Fr 005
Enter.	[Σ+]	6.00
c. Third group.	15.8 [2nd] **Frq** 10 [Σ+]	16.00
d. Fourth group.	16.01 [2nd] **Frq** 12 [Σ+]	28.00
e. Fifth group.	16.7 [Σ+]	29.00
f. Sixth group.	17 [Σ+]	30.00
4. Compute mean.	[ȳ]	15.86
5. Compute standard deviation with n − 1 weighting.	[σn-1]	0.38
6. Calculate variance.	[2nd] x^2	0.14

For this example, the average weight is slightly less than a pound with a standard deviation of .38 pounds and a variance of .14 pounds.

Population

The company's personnel department has recently given an office skills test to the 10 members of your clerical staff. The test scores are in and you want to find the mean, standard deviation, and variance. The scores were 4, 5, 5, 5, 6, 7, 7, 8, 9, 9 out of a possible score of 10.

Procedure	Press	Display
1. Clear calculator and mode registers; select two decimal places.	ON/c 2nd **CLmode** 2nd **Fix** 2	0.00
2. Press 2nd **Mode** until the "STAT" indicator is displayed.	2nd **Mode**	0.00
3. Enter data.		
a. First score.	4 Σ+	1.00
b. Second group.		
Score.	5	5
Number.	2nd **Frq** 3	Fr 003
Enter.	Σ+	4.00
c. Third group.	6 Σ+	5.00
d. Fourth group.	7 2nd **Frq** 2 Σ+	7.00
e. Fifth group.	8 Σ+	8.00
f. Last group.	9 2nd **Frq** 2 Σ+	10.00
4. Compute mean.	ȳ	6.50
5. Compute standard deviation with n weighting.	σn	1.69
6. Calculate variance.	2nd x^2	2.85

The average score is 6.5, and the standard deviation is 1.69. This means that the majority of your test scores fall within the range of 6.5 ± 1.69. The variance (the square of the standard deviation) is 2.85.

Notice that the key σn is used to find the standard deviation with n weighting because the calculations involve the entire population (your clerical staff).

Two Variables

The daily sales for a recent week are shown for two stores,
A and B. What is the average daily sales, standard deviation,
and variance for each store.

	Sales	
	Store A (x)	Store B (y)
Monday	$510	$500
Tuesday	620	510
Wednesday	630	590
Thursday	630	590
Friday	640	750
Saturday	680	800

Note: When you are working with two-variable data, x is
entered before y. After the calculations are completed, the
calculator displays the result for the y value first. You can
also use the **Frq** key to enter data pairs when the same set
of points occur more than once.

Procedure	Press	Display
1. Clear calculator and mode registers; select two decimal places.	ON/c 2nd CLmode 2nd Fix 2	0.00
2. Press 2nd **Mode** until the "STAT" indicator is displayed.	2nd **Mode**	0.00
3. Enter data pairs.		
a. Monday's sales.		
Store A (x).	510 x:y	0.00
Store B (y).	500 Σ+	1.00
b. Tuesday's sales.	620 x:y 510	
	Σ+	2.00

(continued)

(continued)

Procedure	Press	Display
c. Wednesday and Thursday's Sales.		
Store (A).	630 $\boxed{x:y}$	**620.00**
Store (B).	590 $\boxed{2nd}$ **Frq** 2 $\boxed{\Sigma+}$	**4.00**
d. Friday's sales.	640 $\boxed{x:y}$ 750 $\boxed{\Sigma+}$	**5.00**
e. Saturday's sales.	680 $\boxed{x:y}$ 800 $\boxed{\Sigma+}$	**6.00**
4. Compute mean for store B (y).	$\boxed{\bar{y}}$	**623.33**
5. Compute mean for store A (x).	$\boxed{\bar{x}}$	**618.33**
6. Compute standard deviation with $n-1$ weighting for store B (y).	$\boxed{\sigma n\text{-}1}$	**124.53**
7. Calculate variance for store B (y).	$\boxed{2nd}$ x^2	**15506.67**
8. Compute standard deviation with $n-1$ weighting for store A (x).	$\boxed{\sigma n\text{-}1}\boxed{x:y}$	**57.07**
9. Compute variance for store A (x).	$\boxed{2nd}$ x^2	**3256.67**

For this sample, the average daily sales of $618.33 for store A and $623.33 for store B are similar. However, the estimated standard deviation of $57.07 for store A and $124.53 for store B indicate that store B's sales vary more than store A's do.

Finding Expected Value Standard Deviation, And Variance Using Discrete Probabilities

You are considering an investment that has the following distribution.

Return	Probability of Return Occurring
$ 5000	10%
7000	20%
10000	40%
12000	30%

What is the expected value, standard deviation, and variance?*

Procedure	Press	Display
1. Clear calculator and mode registers; select two decimal places.	[ON/c] [2nd] CLmode [2nd] Fix 2	0.00
2. Press [2nd] **Mode** until the "STAT" indicator is displayed.	[2nd] **Mode**	0.00
3. Enter first return.	5000	5000
4. Enter probability.	[2nd] Frq 10	Fr 010
5. Enter values.	[Σ+]	10.00
6. Repeat steps four, five, and six for each set of values.		
a. Second set.	7000 [2nd] Frq 20 [Σ+]	30.00
b. Third set.	10000 [2nd] Frq 40 [Σ+]	70.00
c. Fourth set.	12000 [2nd] Frq 30 [Σ+]	100.00
7. Calculate expected value.	[ȳ]	9500.00
8. Calculate standard deviation.	[σn]	2291.29
9. Calculate variance.	[2nd] x^2	5250000.0

The expected value is $9,500 with a standard deviation of $2,291.29.

*See Appendix A for formulas.

You have determined that as the number of direct labor hours increases, your company's overhead manufacturing costs also increase. You would like to predict the total overhead costs and the variable overhead costs within the normal production range of 4,000 to 6,000 hours. The following data is a sample of the number of labor hours worked and the actual manufacturing overhead incurred for the last 12 months.

Month	Direct Labor Hours (x)	Manufacturing Overhead ($y)
1	4000	21,050
2	4500	24,010
3	5000	24,800
4	5200	25,820
5	5600	26,730
6	6000	28,150
7	5500	26,585
8	4900	24,640
9	4700	24,030
10	4500	23,595
11	4400	23,104
12	4200	22,440

With this data set, you can develop an overhead cost equation, determine the variable overhead rate per hour, and estimate the total overhead for 5,400 hours of direct labor.

In addition, you can evaluate the accuracy of the cost equation by calculating the correlation coefficient, the index of determination, the standard error of the equation, and the standard error of the variable overhead rate estimate.

**Estimating Costs
With Linear
Regression Analysis**

	Procedure	Press	Display
1.	Clear calculator and mode registers; select two decimal places.	[ON/C] [2nd] **CLmode** [2nd] **Fix** 2	0.00
2.	Press [2nd] **Mode** until the "STAT" indicator is displayed.	[2nd] **Mode**	0.00
3.	Enter data. (Calculator displays current number of data entries.)		
	a. Enter first x value.	4000 [x:y]	0.00
	Enter first y value.	21050 [Σ+]	1.00
	b. Enter second pair of data points.	4500 [x:y] 24010 [Σ+]	2.00
	c. Enter third pair of data points.	5000 [x:y] 24800 [Σ+]	3.00
	d. Continue to enter remaining values as above.		
	e. Enter eleventh pair of data points.	4400 [x:y] 23104 [Σ+]	11.00
	f. Enter twelfth pair of data points.	4200 [x:y] 22440 [Σ+]	12.00
4.	Compute y-intercept of regression line.	[2nd] **Intcp**	8770.88
5.	Compute slope of regression line (variable overhead rate).	[2nd] **Slope**	3.24
6.	Compute correlation coefficient.	[2nd] **Corr**	0.99
7.	Calculate and store index of determination.	[2nd] x^2 [STO] 1	0.98
8.	Enter number of data points entered.	12 [STO] 2	12.00 (continued)

(continued)

Procedure	Press	Display
9. Calculate standard error of regression line, using number of pairs of points entered previously.	1 [−] [RCL] 1	
	[=] [STO] 1	0.02
	[Σn] [2nd] x^2	
	[×] [RCL] 1	
	[=] [STO] 1	89470.27
	[RCL] 2 [EXC] 1	
	[×] [RCL] 1 [=]	1073643.2
	[EXC] 1 [−] 2	
	[=]	10.00
	[1/x] [×] [RCL] 1	
	[=] [√x] [STO] 1	327.66
10. Calculate standard error of slope, using number of pairs of points entered previously.	[Σn] [x:y] [2nd] x^2	338541.67
	[×] [RCL] 2	
	[=] [√x]	2015.56
	[1/x] [×] [RCL] 1	
	[=]	.16
11. Estimate y value for a given x value.		
a. Enter x value (number of hours).	5400	5400
b. Compute y value (overhead).	[2nd] **Fcst Y**	26281.97

Using the results for slope (step 5) and y-intercept (step 4), gives the following equation for the manufacturing overhead:

Overhead Cost = 3.24 (Direct Labor Hours) + 8770.88

The variable overhead rate is $3.24 per hour, and the y-intercept of the line is $8,770.88. Since the index of determination (0.98) is a value close to one, you could assume that the equation is a good predictor of the data points within the relevant range of 4,000 to 6,000 hours. (An index of determination close to zero would indicate that the data does not fit the equation well, which means the equation is not a good predictor.)

The value for the standard error of the regression line, $327.66, means that the actual overhead costs will usually equal the estimated costs $\pm 2 \times 327.66. The smaller the standard error, the more accurate your estimate.

The standard error of the slope (.16) indicates that the actual variable overhead rate will usually be equal to $3.24 $\pm$ $2 \times .16$. The smaller this error value, the more accurate your estimate.

For 5,400 hours of direct labor, the equation predicts a total overhead amount of $26,281.97. By applying the standard error of the regression line, the actual amount would usually fall within the range of $26,281.97 $\pm$ $2 \times 327.66 or $25,626.65 to $26,937.25.

Note: To obtain valid estimates when you are making predictions with your calculator, the x values entered for any projections must be within the original range of x data points.

*See Appendix A for the formulas.

A learning curve analysis can be used when labor hours decline by a constant percentage when production doubles. There are, however, *two* learning curve models widely used in industry. One model called the *linear unit model* assumes that the *number of labor hours per unit* decreases by a constant percentage when production quantities double. The second model called the *linear cumulative average model* assumes that the *cumulative average labor hours per unit* decreases by a constant percentage when production quantities double. Both models are illustrated in the following applications.

The learning curve ($y = ax^b$) has many applications in modern business, such as scheduling production, projecting unit costs and labor hours, and setting cost and labor standards. More specifically, learning curve analysis can predict whether or not the number of units produced affects the cumulative average time required to produce each unit. If a good relationship exists, the average time needed decreases as the number of units produced increases.

The equations for the *Linear unit learning curve model* are:

$$Z = ax^b$$

where: Z = number of labor hours required to produce the xth unit

a = number of labor hours needed to produce the first unit

x = number of units produced

b = learning rate factor expressed as

$$\frac{Ln \text{ (Learning rate)}}{Ln \text{ (2)}}$$

The approximate number of hours required to produce x units is expressed as:

$$\text{Total hours} = \frac{a\,[(x + .5)^{1 + b} - .5^{1 + b}]}{1 + b}$$

While the average cumulative hours to produce x units is:

$$\text{Cumulative Average hours} = \frac{\text{Total hours}}{x}$$

The equations for the *Linear Cumulative Average learning curve module* are:

$$y = ax^b$$

where: y = average number of labor hours required for production of x cumulative units

a = number of labor hours needed to produce the first unit

x = number of units produced

b = learning rate factor expressed as

$$\frac{\ln (\text{learning rate})}{\ln(2)}$$

The total number of hours required to produce x units is expressed as:

$$yx = ax^{b+1}$$

while the incremental hours required to produce the xth unit are:

$$\text{man hours} = a(b + 1)x^b$$

Determining the Number of Hours to Produce Units—Cumulative Average Learning Curve Model

Your company manufactures a labor intensive product. The time required to produce the first unit was 352.33 hours. Based on past experience, you have an 80% learning curve effect on the *average cumulative hours* required to complete a unit.

With an 80% learning rate, calculate the following:

       (a) average number of hours to produce 100 units

       (b) number of hours to produce the 100th unit

       (c) total number of hours to produce 100 units

If the memory indicator does not show at least two data memories available, press [2nd] CP before entering the solution.

Procedure	Press	Display
1. Clear calculator and mode registers; select two decimal places.	[ON/C] [2nd] CLmode [2nd] Fix 2	0.00
2. Press [2nd] **Mode** until the "FIN" indicator is displayed.	[2nd] **Mode**	0.00
3. Enter learning rate; calculate and store learning rate factor (b).	80 [%] [2nd] **lnx** [÷] 2 [2nd] **lnx** [=] [STO] 1	−0.32
4. Enter number of units (x) you want to produce and calculate x^b.	100 [2nd] y^x [RCL] 1 [=]	0.23
5. Multiply by time required to build first unit (a) to calculate average number of hours to produce x (100) units.	[X] 352.33 [=] [STO] 2	80.00
6. Calculate hours required to build 100th unit.	1 [+] [RCL] 1 [X] [RCL] 2 [=]	54.25
7. Multiply by number of units to calculate total number of hours needed to produce the first x (100) units.	[RCL] 2 [X] 100 [=]	8000.06

With this procedure, you can easily perform a sensitivity analysis to determine the effects on your project from various estimations of your learning rate and the time required to build the first unit, as well as predicting the learning curve values.

Reference: "*The Learning Curve as a Production Tool*," Harvard Business Review.

Learning Curve Analysis

Determining the Number of Hours to Produce Units—Linear Unit Learning Curve Model

Your company manufactures a labor intensive product. The time required to produce the first unit was 500 hours. Based on past experience, you have an 80% learning curve effect. Each time production doubles, the last unit takes 80% of the hours that the final unit of the prior doubling required. For example, if the 100th unit required 100 hours, the 200th unit requires 80 hours.

With an 80% learning rate, calculate the following:

(a) number of hours to produce the 100th unit
(b) total number of hours to produce 100 units
(c) average number of hours to produce 100 units

Note: The procedure shown below for determining cumulative hours for the linear unit model is an approximation and there will be a small difference when compared to tables.

If the memory indicator does not show at least four data memories available, press [2nd] CP before entering the solution.

Procedure	Press	Display
1. Clear calculator and mode registers; select two decimal places.	[ON/c] [2nd] **CLmode** [2nd] **Fix 2**	**0.00**
2. Press [2nd] **Mode** until the "FIN" indicator is displayed.	[2nd] **Mode**	**0.00**
3. Enter learning rate; calculate and store.	80 [%] [2nd] **lnx** [÷] 2 [2nd] **lnx** [=] [STO] 1	**– 0.32**
4. Add one and store.	[+] 1 [=] [STO] 2	**0.68**
5. Enter and store number of units (x) you want to produce and calculate x^b.	100 [STO] 3 [2nd] y^x [RCL] 1 [=]	**0.23**
6. Multiply by time required to produce first unit (a) to calculate number of hours (z) to make the 100th (x) unit and store.	[X] 500 [PV] [=]	**113.53**
7. Calculate approximation of future cumulative hours to make 100 (x) units.	.5 [2nd] y^x [RCL] 2 [=] [STO] 4 [RCL] 3 [+] .5 [=] [2nd] y^x [RCL] 2 [−] [RCL] 4 [÷] [RCL] 2 [X] [RCL] [PV] [=]	**16339.04**
8. Calculate average cumulative hours.	[÷] [RCL] 3 [=]	**163.39**

The approximation for cumulative average hours is 163.39 hours and the number of hours required to produce the 100th unit is 113.53 hours.

Determining the Learning Curve Rate

The technique shown below is valid for both the linear unit model and the cumulative average model. The example solves for the learning curve rate assuming the cumulative average model. To solve for the learning curve rate under the linear unit model, simply use the hours required to build the xth unit for the y value; the y value is the incremented hours for the xth unit.

A company has started a new product line and has made the following observations.

Cumulative Units Produced (x)	Average Cumulative Labor Hours Per Unit (y)
50	31
80	24
100	22
125	19.50
160	17.30

Is there a learning curve relationship? If so, what is the learning rate, and how many hours did it take to produce the first unit? Assume the cumulative average learning curve model is used.

Procedure	Press	Display
1. Clear calculator and mode registers; select two decimal places.	ON/c 2nd **CLmode** 2nd **Fix 2**	0.00
2. Press 2nd **Mode** until the "STAT" indicator is displayed.	2nd **Mode**	0.00
3. Enter data. (Calculator displays current number of data entries.)		
a. Enter first x value.	50 2nd lnx x:y	0.00
Enter first y value.	31 2nd lnx Σ+	1.00

(continued)

(continued)

Procedure	Press	Display
b. Enter second pair of data points.	80 [2nd] lnx [x:y] 24 [2nd] lnx [Σ+]	2.00
c. Enter third pair of data points.	100 [2nd] lnx [x:y] 22 [2nd] lnx [Σ+]	3.00
d. Enter fourth pair of data points.	125 [2nd] lnx [x:y] 19.50 [2nd] lnx [Σ+]	4.00
e. Enter fifth pair of data points.	160 [2nd] lnx [x:y] 17.30 [2nd] lnx [Σ+]	5.00
4. Compute correlation between x and y values.	[2nd] Corr	− 1.00
5. Calculate number of hours required to produce first units.	[2nd] Intcp [2nd] e^x	216.17
6. Calculate learning rate factor (b).	[2nd] Slope	− 0.50
7. Calculate learning rate as a percentage.	[X] 2 [2nd] lnx [=] [2nd] e^x [X] 100 [=]	70.81

The correlation value of − 1 indicates that a good negative relationship exists. (As the x values increase, the y values decrease proportionally.) The learning rate is 70.81% and the time needed to produce the first unit is 216.17 hours. The 70.81% rate means that each time you double your lot quantity, the average number of cumulative labor hours is 70.81% times the previous cumulative value. In this example, the average cumulative value was 31 hours per unit for the first 50 units produced. For 100 units (2×50), the average cumulative value was 22 hours ($31 \times 70.81\% = 21.95$ hours), indicating that 70.81% is a reasonable learning rate estimate. With these values you can go on to calculate the learning curve values, using the procedure in the previous example.

Forecasting plays an important role today in financial planning. Projecting trends in sales, forecasting financial requirements, and planning production needs and output are only a few of the areas in business that call for sound forecasting techniques. This section contains forecasting programs that can be used here and separately as building blocks for other applications not discussed. While these programs are not exhaustive, they provide basic routines useful in forecasting.

The forecasting program and seasonal index program discussed first assume a multiplicative model.

Forecast value $= T \times S \times C \times I$

where:

T = general trend relationship expressed as a unit value

S = seasonal variations that occur within a year

C = long-run variations that occur over long run periods

I = random variations other than T, S, or C

The values for S and C are expressed as index values. Thus, if you had a situation with the values $T = 515$, $S = 1.05$, $C = 0.99$, the forecast would be:

Forecast value $= 515 \times 1.05 \times 0.99$

$= 535.34$

The programs are used here to estimate the seasonal variation or index value. The trend relationship determined is equal to $T \times C \times I$. This is computed by dividing the original value by S.

Original forecast value = $T \times S \times C \times I$

Value to estimate trend = $\dfrac{T \times S \times C \times I}{S} = T \times C \times I$

The values T, C, and I are used to determine the trend line. Once the trend values are determined, they are used to project a future value, which is then multiplied by the seasonal index to arrive at the forecast value.

Note: The second forecasting method applies exponential smoothing to estimate future values.

Reference: Chisholm & Whitaker, *Forecasting Methods*; and Croxton, Cowden and Bolch, *Practical Business Statistics*.

Applying Linear Regression Analysis to Forecasting

Your company has recently started advertising in a series of magazines on a weekly basis. Your marketing manager figures that the advertising campaign of one week will affect the sales volume of the following week. He has a record of the amount spent on advertising each week (x) and the corresponding sales volume (y). There seems to be a fairly good relationship between the two. What would be the expected sales volume if $1,700 is spent on advertising next week?

Amount Spent On Advertising (x)	Weekly Sales Volume (y)
$1000	$101,000
$1250	$116,000
$1500	$165,000
$2000	$209,000
$2500	$264,000
$1700	???

Procedure	Press	Display
1. Clear calculator and mode registers; select two decimal places.	ON/c 2nd CLmode 2nd Fix 2	0.00
2. Press 2nd Mode until the "STAT" indicator is displayed.	2nd Mode	0.00
3. Enter data. (Calculator displays current number of data entries.)		
a. Enter first x value. Enter first y value.	1000 x:y 101000 Σ+	0.00 1.00
b. Enter second pair of data points.	1250 x:y 116000 Σ+	2.00
c. Enter third pair of data points.	1500 x:y 165000 Σ+	3.00
d. Enter fourth pair of data points.	2000 x:y 209000 Σ+	4.00
e. Enter fifth pair of data points.	2500 x:y 264000 Σ+	5.00
4. Calculate index of determination.	2nd Corr 2nd x^2	0.99
5. Calculate y value for x = $1700.	1700 2nd Fcst Y	176543.10

Since the index of determination (0.99) is close to one, the regression line is a "good fit" to the data. Based on this straight line approximation, the projected weekly sales volume for $1,700 spent on advertising is $176,543.10.

12 STATISTICS

A Trend Line Analysis

A stock that you've been watching has reported the following earnings per share during the past few years:

$1.52 in 1978
1.35 in 1979
1.53 in 1980
2.17 in 1981
3.60 in 1982

You'd like to predict the earnings per share for the next three years. You'd also like to estimate in what year you could expect the earnings per share to reach $6.50.

First, you'll enter your data, using the $\boxed{x:y}\boxed{\Sigma+}$ keys. In this case, the "x" values are a series of years in sequence, and the "y" values are the stock dividends recorded for each year. (Data for a series of successive years are common for trend line analysis situations.)

To make predictons on earnings for future years, just enter the year and press $\boxed{2nd}$ **Fcst Y**.

Procedure	Press	Display
1. Clear calculator and mode registers; select two decimal places.	$\boxed{ON/c}$ $\boxed{2nd}$ **CLmode** $\boxed{2nd}$ **Fix 2**	0.00
2. Press $\boxed{2nd}$ **Mode** until the "STAT" indicator is displayed.	$\boxed{2nd}$ **Mode**	0.00
3. Enter data. (Calculator displays current number of data entries.)	1978 $\boxed{x:y}$ 1.52 $\boxed{\Sigma+}$	1.00
	1.35 $\boxed{\Sigma+}$	2.00
	1.53 $\boxed{\Sigma+}$	3.00
	2.17 $\boxed{\Sigma+}$	4.00
	3.60 $\boxed{\Sigma+}$	5.00
4. Predict earnings for 1983, 1984, 1985.	1983 $\boxed{2nd}$ **Fcst Y**	3.53
	1984 $\boxed{2nd}$ **Fcst Y**	4.03
	1985 $\boxed{2nd}$ **Fcst Y**	4.52

Now, see how well the two sets of data are correlated by pressing $\boxed{2nd}$ **Corr** and finding 0.85, a fairly good correlation.

Three-Point Moving Average

The following program computes a three-point moving average using the following formula.

$$\text{moving average} = \frac{\text{Point } i + \text{Point } (i + 1) + \text{Point } (i + 2)}{3}$$

Beginning with points 1, 2, and 3, then 2, 3, and 4, etc., the resulting moving-average value for each triad of points can be plotted.

The following program simplifies the calculation of each point.

The procedure for entering this program is shown in the following example. Refer to the "Programming Keys" section of chapter 1 for additional information on programming procedures.

Step	Keystroke	Key Code	Step	Keystroke	Key Code
	[2nd] CP		08	[RCL]	71
	[LRN]		09	[2]	02
00	[EXC]	91	10	[÷]	55
01	[2]	02	11	[3]	03
02	[EXC]	91	12	[=]	95
03	[1]	01	13	[R/S]	13
04	[+]	85	14	[2nd] RST	37
05	[RCL]	71		[LRN]	
06	[1]	01		[2nd] RST	
07	[+]	85			

Example: Clothing sales from a local chain department store are as follows.

Month	3-Month Sales (in $000)	Moving Average
January	105	
February	110	110.00
March	115	115.00
April	120	117.67
May	118	117.67
June	115	114.33
July	110	111.00
August	108	109.61
September	111	111.33
October	115	116.00
November	122	115.33
December	109	

The three-point moving averages calculated on the next page are also shown here. Note that the average on any three points actually applies to the center point of the three.

Procedure	Press	Display
1. Clear calculator and mode registers; select two decimal places.	ON/C 2nd **CLmode** 2nd **Fix** 2	0.00
2. Press 2nd **Mode** until the "FIN" indicator is displayed.	2nd **Mode**	0.00
3. Enter three point moving average program as listed on page **12**-25.		
4. Clear memories and reset.	2nd **CLmem** 2nd **RST**	0.00
5. Enter first data point.	105 STO 1	**105.00**
6. Enter second data point.	110 STO 2	**110.00**
7. Enter next data point and calculate moving average.	115 R/S	**110.00**
Repeat step seven for each data point.		
	120 R/S	**115.00**
	118 R/S	**117.67**
	115 R/S	**117.67**
	110 R/S	**114.33**
	108 R/S	**111.00**
	111 R/S	**109.67**
	115 R/S	**111.33**
	122 R/S	**116.00**
	109 R/S	**115.33**

Reference: Croxton, Cowden, and Bolch, *Practical Business Statistics.*

Four-Point Centered Moving Average

As with the three-point moving average, the four-point centered moving average can be used to "smooth" data, thus minimizing periodic variations. Each application of this type of averaging produces the following:

moving average =

$$\frac{\text{Point } i + 2(\text{Point } (i + l) + \text{Point } (i + 2) + \text{Point } (i + 3) + \text{Point } (i + 4)}{8}$$

What actually happens is that two four-point averages are taken and summed together.

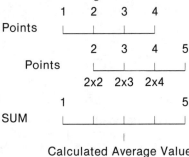

Calculated Average Value

The procedure for entering this program is shown in the following example. Refer to the "Programming Keys" section of chapter 1 for additional information on programming procedures.

Step	Keystroke	Key Code	Step	Keystroke	Key Code
	[2nd] CP		18	[÷]	55
	[LRN]		19	[2]	02
00	[x:y]	51	20	[+]	85
01	[RCL]	71	21	[RCL]	71
02	[%i]	22	22	[%i]	22
03	[N]	21	23	[+]	85
04	[RCL]	71	24	[RCL]	71
05	[PMT]	23	25	[PMT]	23
06	[%i]	22	26	[+]	85
07	[RCL]	71	27	[RCL]	71
08	[PV]	24	28	[PV]	24
09	[PMT]	23	29	[÷]	55
10	[RCL]	71	30	[4]	04
11	[FV]	25	31	[=]	95
12	[PV]	24	32	[2nd] Print	99
13	[x:y]	51	33	[R/S]	13
14	[FV]	25	34	[2nd] RST	37
15	[+]	85		[LRN]	
16	[RCL]	71		[2nd] RST	
17	[N]	21			

Example: A diaper company had the following quarterly sales (in $000) over 4 years.

	Quarter			
Years	1	2	3	4
1974	370	389	440	510
1975	395	410	485	545
1976	428	445	520	575
1977	460	480	550	610

Calculate a four-point moving average for these sales.

Procedure	Press	Display
1. Clear calculator and mode registers; select two decimal places.	[ON/c] [2nd] **CLmode** [2nd] **Fix** 2	0.00
2. Press [2nd] **Mode** until the "FIN" indicator is displayed.	[2nd] **Mode**	0.00
3. Enter program as found on previous page.		
4. Clear memory and reset.	[2nd] **CLmem** [2nd] **RST**	0.00
5. Enter first data point.	370 [%i]	370.00
6. Enter second data point.	389 [PMT]	389.00
7. Enter third data point.	440 [PV]	440.00
8. Enter fourth data point.	510 [FV]	510.00
9. Start program; enter next data point and calculate average for current four points.	395 [R/S]	430.38
	410 [R/S]	436.13
	485 [R/S]	444.38
	545 [R/S]	454.38
	428 [R/S]	462.88
	445 [R/S]	471.38
	520 [R/S]	480.13
	575 [R/S]	488.25
	460 [R/S]	496.00
	480 [R/S]	504.38
	550 [R/S]	512.50
	610 [R/S]	520.63

Below is a summary of these quarterly sales.

	Quarter			
Years	1	2	3	4
1974			430.38	436.13
1975	444.38	454.38	462.88	471.38
1976	480.13	488.25	496.00	504.38
1977	512.50	520.63		

Reference: Croxton, Cowden, and Bolch, *Practical Business Statistics*.

STATISTICS **12**

Seasonal Index Using Ratio to Centered Moving Average

Seasonal index values can be determined by the ratio of periodic sales to a four-point centered moving average to annual sales.

1. Compute a four-point moving average for the periodic data using the "Four-Point Centered Moving Average" program.
2. Divide each periodic value by its associated average calculated above yielding a periodic ratio.
3. Compute the average of these periodic ratios for each quarter to determine the seasonal index.

Example: Compute the seasonal index values for the following quarterly sales data (in $000).

	Quarter			
Years	1	2	3	4
1979	450	486	553	583
1980	453	488	562	593
1981	476	517	588	614
1982	482	524	607	623

The four-point moving average program run on this data produces the following weighted average values.

	Quarter			
Years	1	2	3	4
1979			518.38	519.00
1980	520.38	522.75	526.88	533.38
1981	540.25	546.13	549.50	551.13
1982	554.38	557.88		

If the memory indicator does not show at least four data memories available, press [2nd] **CP** before entering the solution.

Forecasting

Procedure	Press	Display
1. Clear calculator and select two decimal places.	[2nd] **CLmem** [2nd] **Fix** 2	**0.00**
2. Press [2nd] **Mode** until the "FIN" indicator is displayed.	[2nd] **Mode**	**0.00**
3. Divide each quarter's data by the weighted average for that quarter.*		
1979 – Q3	553 [÷] 518.38 [=] [SUM] 3	**1.07**
1979 – Q4	583 [÷] 519 [=] [SUM] 4	**1.12**
1980 – Q1	453 [÷] 520.38 [=] [SUM] 1	**0.87**
1980 – Q2	488 [÷] 522.75 [=] [SUM] 2	**0.93**
1980 – Q3	562 [÷] 526.88 [=] [SUM] 3	**1.07**
1980 – Q4	593 [÷] 533.38 [=] [SUM] 4	**1.11**
1981 – Q1	476 [÷] 540.25 [=] [SUM] 1	**0.88**
1981 – Q2	517 [÷] 546.13 [=] [SUM] 2	**0.95**
1981 – Q3	588 [÷] 549.5 [=] [SUM] 3	**1.07**
1981 – Q4	614 [÷] 551.13 [=] [SUM] 4	**1.11**
1982 – Q1	482 [÷] 554.38 [=] [SUM] 1	**0.87**
1982 – Q2	524 [÷] 557.88 [=] [SUM] 2	**0.94**

(continued)

(continued)

Procedure	Press	Display
5. Calculate the seasonal index values.		
First quarter	[RCL] 1 [÷] 3	
	[=]	**0.87**
Second quarter	[RCL] 2 [÷] 3	
	[=]	**0.94**
Third quarter	[RCL] 3 [÷] 3	
	[=]	**1.07**
Fourth quarter	[RCL] 4 [÷] 3	
	[=]	**1.12**

Remember to divide the accumulation of the index by the number of observations for each quarter as was done in step three.

Note: For simplicity the results above have been rounded to two decimal places. For greater accuracy, however, you may want to display and use more significant digits for your seasonal indexes. Also, the sum of the indexes should always equal the number of seasonal periods with which you are working (in this case, four).

*Press [2nd] **CLmem** before running a second application of this program.

References: Croxton, Cowden, and Bolch, *Practical Business Statistics*. Parsons, *Statistical Analysis*.

12

Seasonal Index Using Ratio to Yearly Sales Method

Seasonal index values can be determined by the ratio of periodic sales to yearly sales.

1. Find the average sales per period (usually a quarter).
2. Divide average sales per period by the average sales per year.
3. Average the ratios from the first period of each year to get the seasonal index for that period. Repeat for each period.

Example: Compute the seasonal index for each quarter of the sales data (in $000) shown below.

	Quarter			
Years	1	2	3	4
1979	450	486	553	583
1980	453	488	562	593
1981	476	517	588	614
1982	482	524	607	623

Procedure	Press	Display
1. Clear calculator and mode registers; select two decimal places.	[ON/c] [2nd] **CLmode** [2nd] **Fix** 2	**0.00**
2. Press [2nd] **Mode** until the "STAT" indicator is displayed.	[2nd] **Mode**	**0.00**
3. Calculate average sales for each year.		
a. 1979 data.	450 [Σ+]	**1.00**
	486 [Σ+]	**2.00**
	553 [Σ+]	**3.00**
	583 [Σ+]	**4.00**
Average for 1979.	[ȳ]	**518.00**
b. 1980 data.	[2nd] **CLmode**	
	453 [Σ+]	**1.00**
	488 [Σ+]	**2.00**
	562 [Σ+]	**3.00**
	593 [Σ+]	**4.00**
Average for 1980.	[ȳ]	**524.00**
c. 1981 data.	[2nd] **CLmode**	
	476 [Σ+]	**1.00**
	517 [Σ+]	**2.00**
	588 [Σ+]	**3.00**
	614 [Σ+]	**4.00**
Average for 1981.	[ȳ]	**548.75**
d. 1982 data.	[2nd] **CLmode**	
	482 [Σ+]	**1.00**
	524 [Σ+]	**2.00**
	607 [Σ+]	**3.00**
	623 [Σ+]	**4.00**
Average for 1982.	[ȳ]	**559.00**

The next step is computing the index based on each year's sales and accumulate the first quarter ratios in memory one, second quarter in memory two, etc.

If the memory indicator does not show at least four data memories available, press [2nd] **CP** before entering the solution.

Procedure	Press	Display
1. Clear calculator, mode registers, and memories; select two decimal places.	[ON/c] [2nd] **CLmode** [2nd] **CLmem** [2nd] **Fix** 2	0.00
2. Press [2nd] **Mode** until the "FIN" indicator is displayed.	[2nd] **Mode**	0.00
3. Enter average yearly sales starting with the first year (1979).	[÷] [2nd] K 518 [=]	0.00
4. Enter the quarterly sales for the year (1979).		
Q1	450 [=] [STO] 1	0.87
Q2	486 [=] [STO] 2	0.94
Q3	553 [=] [STO] 3	1.07
Q4	583 [=] [STO] 4	1.13
5. Repeat steps three and four for each year.		
Average Sales 1980.	[÷] [2nd] K 524 [=]	0.00
Q1	453 [=] [SUM] 1	0.86
Q2	488 [=] [SUM] 2	0.93
Q3	562 [=] [SUM] 3	1.07
Q4	593 [=] [SUM] 4	1.13
Average Sales 1981.	[÷] [2nd] K 548.75 [=]	0.00
Q1	476 [=] [SUM] 1	0.87
Q2	517 [=] [SUM] 2	0.94
Q3	588 [=] [SUM] 3	1.07
Q4	614 [=] [SUM] 4	1.12

(continued)

(continued)

Procedure	Press	Display
Average Sales 1982.	[÷] [2nd] K 559	
	[=]	**0.00**
Q1	482 [=] [SUM] 1	**0.86**
Q2	524 [=] [SUM] 2	**0.94**
Q3	607 [=] [SUM] 3	**1.09**
Q4	623 [=] [SUM] 4	**1.11**

6. Calculate seasonal indexes for:

First quarter.	[RCL] 1 [÷] 4	
	[=]	**0.87**
Second quarter.	[RCL] 2 [÷] 4	
	[=]	**0.94**
Third quarter.	[RCL] 3 [÷] 4	
	[=]	**1.07**
Fourth quarter.	[RCL] 4 [÷] 4	
	[=]	**1.12**

Remember to divide the accumulation of indexes by the total number of observations for that quarter as was done in step five.

Trend Projections (Forecasting) Using Seasonal Indexes

Once the seasonal indexes have been determined for a set of information, projection of future events (sales, growth, etc.) can easily be made using the regression capabilities built into your calculator. The existing data are first deseasonalized to make projections more accurate, then reseasonalized to obtain the forecast values.

1. Deseasonalize the information from each period of each year by dividing each by the seasonal index of that period.
2. Enter the deseasonalized data into the regression routine. You can find the slope, intercept and correlation coefficient if you want to analyze the data.
3. Now future information can be projected.
4. Seasonalize the data for the actual forecast.

Example: Forecast 1978 quarterly sales based on the following historical data (in $000).

| | **Quarter** | | | |
Years	1	2	3	4
1979	450	486	553	583
1980	453	488	562	593
1981	476	517	588	614
1982	482	524	607	623
Seasonal Indexes	0.87	0.94	1.07	1.12

The quarterly sales are deseasonalized using the procedure shown below.

Procedure	Press	Display
1. Clear calculator and mode registers; select two decimal places.	[ON/c] [2nd] **CLmode** [2nd] **Fix** 2	0.00
2. Enter first period index (First quarter).	[÷] [2nd] K .87 [=]	0.00
3. Enter first period sales for each year and calculate deseasonalized sales.		
1979	450 [=]	517.24
1980	453 [=]	520.69
1981	476 [=]	547.13
1982	482 [=]	554.02
4. Repeat steps two and three for each period (quarter).		
a. Second quarter index.	[ON/c] [÷] [2nd] K .94 [=]	0.00
Sales for second quarter.		
1979	486 [=]	517.02
1980	488 [=]	519.15
1981	517 [=]	550.00
1982	524 [=]	557.45

b. Third quarter index. ON/c ÷ 2nd K

	1.07 =	**0.00**
1979	553 =	**516.82**
1980	562 =	**525.23**
1981	588 =	**549.53**
1982	607 =	**567.29**

c. Fourth quarter index. ON/c ÷ 2nd K

	1.12 =	**0.00**

Sales for fourth quarter.

1979	583 =	**520.54**
1980	593 =	**529.46**
1981	614 =	**548.21**
1982	623 =	**556.25**

The deseasonalized data is now summarized below. Note: enter the data in calendar order, not in the order as calculated above.

	Quarter			
Years	1	2	3	4
1979	517.24	517.02	516.82	520.54
1980	520.69	519.15	525.23	529.46
1981	547.13	550.00	549.53	548.21
1982	554.02	557.45	567.29	556.25

Forecasting

12 STATISTICS

The next step is calculating the trend line and projecting the future estimates using the calculator's internal regression routines.

Procedure	Press	Display
1. Clear calculator and mode registers; select two decimal places.	[ON/c] [2nd] CLmode [2nd] Fix 2	0.00
2. Press [2nd] **Mode** until the "STAT" indicator is displayed.	[2nd] **Mode**	0.00
3. Enter the first period number (usually one).	1 [x:y]	0.00
4. Enter deseasonal values in order of occurence.		
1979 – Q1	517.24 [Σ+]	1.00
Q2	517.02 [Σ+]	2.00
Q3	516.82 [Σ+]	3.00
Q4	520.54 [Σ+]	4.00
1980 – Q1	520.69 [Σ+]	5.00
Q2	519.15 [Σ+]	6.00
Q3	525.23 [Σ+]	7.00
Q4	529.46 [Σ+]	8.00
1981 – Q1	547.13 [Σ+]	9.00
Q2	550.00 [Σ+]	10.00
Q3	549.53 [Σ+]	11.00
Q4	548.21 [Σ+]	12.00
1982 – Q1	554.02 [Σ+]	13.00
Q2	557.45 [Σ+]	14.00
Q3	567.29 [Σ+]	15.00
Q4	556.25 [Σ+]	16.00
5. Calculate intercept.	[2nd] **Intcp**	506.96
6. Calculate slope.	[2nd] **Slope**	3.56
7. Calculate correlation coefficient.	[2nd] **Corr**	0.95

(continued)

12-40

(continued)

Procedure	Press	Display
8. Calculate future estimates by entering future period number. Sixteen periods of data have been entered, so the first period of 1983 is 17, the second period is 18, etc.	17 [2nd] **Fcst Y**	**567.54**
9. Reseasonalize new point by multiplying by appropriate quarterly index.	[×] .87 [=]	**493.76**
10. Repeat steps eight and nine for each forecasted period.	18 [2nd] **Fcst Y**	**571.11**
	[×] .94 [=]	**536.84**
	19 [2nd] **Fcst Y**	**574.67**
	[×] 1.07 [=]	**614.90**
	20 [2nd] **Fcst Y**	**578.24**
	[×] 1.12 [=]	**647.62**

The projected sales for 1978 are:

Quarter	Sales
1	493.76
2	536.84
3	614.90
4	647.62

The above technique can be used with any type of statistically derived trend line, but the assumptions underlying the data used should be closely evaluated. Be sure the relationships being made are valid and that the data satisfy the statistical assumptions. Another problem in forecasting is auto correlation or serial correlation. For a description of these problems refer to a textbook on statistical forecasting.

Determining Alpha Using Historical Data

Exponential smoothing is a forecasting method similar to a weighted average but eliminates keeping track of individual observations. To use this technique, you need an estimate of the smoothing constant alpha. This constant is a value between zero and one that serves as the weighting factor. The value of alpha determines how much the current information influences the forecast value. The closer alpha is to one, the greater the weight of the most recent period in the forecast. A weight of (1 − alpha) is given to preceding periods. If you want the exponential smoothing factor to be equivalent to forecasts that would be obtained by using a moving average with n observations, let alpha = 2/(n + 1).

The equations used in this application are:

$$S_t = \text{alpha} \, (X_t - S_{t-1}) + S_{t-1}$$
$$T_t = \text{alpha} \, (S_t - S_{t-1} - T_{t-1}) + T_{t-1}$$
$$D_{t+1} = S_t + \frac{(1 - \text{alpha})}{\text{alpha}} \, T_t$$
$$\text{sigma } e^2 = \text{sigma} \, (D_{t+1} - X_{t+1})$$

where:

$\quad$ alpha = smoothing constant $0 < \text{alpha} < 1$

$\quad S_t$ = the moving (smoothed) average of the observations in time period t.

$\quad X_t$ = the input value for period t.

$\quad T_t$ = the projected trend value of period t + 1

$\quad D_{t+1}$ = the forecast value for period t + 1

sigma e^2 = the cumulative squared error between the forecast value and the actual value.

The best value of alpha minimizes the cumulative squared error. The value is found by trying several alpha values on the historical data to find the alpha value that generates the smallest cumulative squared error. As a result, two steps are necessary for forecasting with exponential smoothing. First, determine an appropriate alpha value using historical data. Second, using the alpha, S_{t-1}, and T_{t-1} values from the first step forecast the next period. For subsequent periods, only the revised values of S_{t-1} and T_{t-1} and the alpha coefficient are necessary to determine the forecast values.

Forecasting With Exponential Smoothing

The initial value for S_{t-1} when using historical data can be determined by either taking an average of prior values or using the first historical data point. An initial estimate for T_{t-1} using prior values can be found using:

$$T_{t-1} = (X_{t-1} - S_{t-1}) \times \frac{alpha}{1 - alpha}$$

When working with seasonal data, the data should be deseasonalized and the seasonal indexes determined before applying exponential smoothing. The projected D_{t-1} value is multiplied by its seasonal index to determine the seasonalized forecast.

Example: ABC's deseasonalized sales data and seasonal indexes for 1980, 1981, and 1982 are given below. Compute the values for alpha, S_{t-1} and T_{t-1} necessary to forecast the first quarter sales for 1983.

	Quarter			
Years	1	2	3	4
1980	520.69	519.15	525.23	529.46
1981	547.13	550.00	549.53	548.21
1982	554.02	557.45	567.29	556.25
Seasonal Index	0.87	0.94	1.07	1.12

Since the indexes were determined using quarterly data, a reasonable first guess for alpha is found using an alpha equivalent to a four point centered moving average.

alpha $= 2/(8 + 1) = .22$

The initial value for S_{t-1} is the average sales using the 1980 sales data.

$S_{t-1} = (520.69 + 519.15 + 525.23 + 529.46)/4$
$= 523.63$

The initial trend value is found using:

$$T_{t-1} = (547.13 - 523.63) \frac{.22}{1 - .22}$$

$= 6.63$

Reference: Clark and Schkade. *Statistical Analysis for Administration Decisions.* 2nd ed.

The following program is used to compute the forecast based on historical data.

The procedure for entering this program is shown in the following example. Refer to the "Programming Keys" section of chapter 1 for additional information on programming procedures.

Step	Keystroke	Key Code	Step	Keystroke	Key Code
	2nd CP		17	FV	25
	LRN		18	X	65
00	−	75	19	RCL	71
01	RCL	71	20	%i	22
02	PV	24	21	+	85
03	X	65	22	RCL	71
04	RCL	71	23	FV	25
05	%i	22	24	X	65
06	+	85	25	FV	25
07	RCL	71	26	RCL	71
08	PV	24	27	PMT	23
09	+	85	28	+	85
10	RCL	71	29	RCL	71
11	PV	24	30	PV	24
12	+/−	94	31	=	95
13	x:y	51	32	R/S	13
14	PV	24	33	2nd RST	37
15	−	75		LRN	
16	RCL	71		2nd RST	

Procedure	Press	Display
1. Clear calculator and mode registers; select two decimal places.	ON/c 2nd CLmode 2nd Fix 2	0.00
2. Press 2nd Mode until the "FIN" indicator is displayed.	2nd Mode	0.00
3. Enter program.		
4. Clear mode registers and reset program.	2nd CLmode 2nd RST	0.00

(continued)

(continued)

Procedure	Press	Display
5. Enter initial value for smoothing factor S_{t-1}.	523.63 $\boxed{PV}$	**523.63**
6. Enter initial trend value T_{t-1}.	6.63 $\boxed{FV}$	**6.63**
7. Enter alpha.	.22 $\boxed{\%i}$	**0.22**
8. Calculate and enter $(1 - alpha)/alpha$.	$\boxed{+/-}\boxed{+}$ 1 $\boxed{÷}$ $\boxed{RCL}\boxed{\%i}\boxed{=}\boxed{PMT}$	**3.55**
9. Enter first historical value; 1981 first quarter.	547.13	**547.13**
Reset program and calculate forecast value for next period.	$\boxed{2nd}$ **RST** $\boxed{R/S}$	**551.17**
10. Enter second value for 1981 second quarter and calculate error.	$\boxed{-}$ 550 $\boxed{=}$	**1.17**
a. Square error and store.	$\boxed{2nd}$ x^2 $\boxed{N}$	**1.36**
b. Enter second value and calculate forecast value for 1981 third quarter.	550 $\boxed{R/S}$	**554.55**
11. 1981 fourth quarter forecast.		
a. Enter 1981 third quarter value and calculate error and sum.	$\boxed{-}$ 549.53 $\boxed{=}$ $\boxed{2nd}$ x^2 $\boxed{+}\boxed{RCL}\boxed{N}$ $\boxed{=}\boxed{N}$	**26.55**
b. Enter 1981 third quarter value and calculate 1981 fourth quarter forecast.	549.53 $\boxed{R/S}$	**556.20**

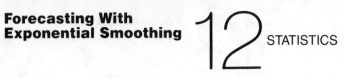
(continued)

Procedure	Press	Display

Repeat step 11 for each historical value.

12. 1982 first quarter forecast.

    a. Enter 1981, fourth quarter value and calculate error.
$\boxed{-}$ 548.21 $\boxed{=}$
$\boxed{2nd}$ x^2
$\boxed{+}$ $\boxed{RCL}$ $\boxed{N}$
$\boxed{=}$ $\boxed{N}$ **90.41**

    b. Enter 1981, fourth quarter value and calculate 1982 first quarter forecast.
548.21 $\boxed{R/S}$ **556.37**

13. 1982 second quarter forecast.

    a. Enter 1982 first quarter value and calculate error.
$\boxed{-}$ 554.02 $\boxed{=}$
$\boxed{2nd}$ x^2 $\boxed{+}$
$\boxed{RCL}$ $\boxed{N}$ $\boxed{=}$ $\boxed{N}$ **95.92**

    b. Enter 1982 first quarter value and calculate 1982 second quarter forecast.
554.02 $\boxed{R/S}$ **558.35**

14. 1982 third quarter forecast.

    a. Enter 1982 second quarter value and calculate error.
$\boxed{-}$ 557.45
$\boxed{=}$ $\boxed{2nd}$ x^2 $\boxed{+}$
$\boxed{RCL}$ $\boxed{N}$ $\boxed{=}$ $\boxed{N}$ **96.73**

    b. Enter 1982 second quarter value and calculate 1982 third quarter forecast.
557.45 $\boxed{R/S}$ **560.69**

15. 1982 fourth quarter forecast.

    a. Enter 1982 third quarter value and calculate error.
$\boxed{-}$ 567.29 $\boxed{=}$
$\boxed{2nd}$ x^2 $\boxed{+}$
$\boxed{RCL}$ $\boxed{N}$ $\boxed{=}$ $\boxed{N}$ **140.32**

(continued)

(continued)

Procedure	Press	Display
b. Enter 1982 third quarter value and calculate 1982 fourth quarter forecast.	567.29 [R/S]	**565.81**
16. 1983 first quarter forecast.		
a. Enter 1982 fourth quarter value and calculate error.	[−] 556.25 [=] [2nd] x^2 [+] [RCL][N][=][N]	**231.66**
b. Enter 1982 fourth quarter value and calculate 1983 first quarter forecast.	556.25 [R/S]	**564.67**
17. Multiply deseasonalized forecast by appropriate seasonal index to determine seasonalized sales.	[×] .87 [=]	**491.26**
18. Recall squared error.	[RCL][N]	**231.66**
19. Recall seasonal smoothing factor S_{t-1}.	[RCL][PV]	**551.86**
20. Recall trend factor T_{t-1}.	[RCL][FV]	**3.61**
21. Recall alpha.	[RCL][%i]	**0.22**

The seasonalized forecast for 1983 quarter 1 is 491.26.

Using an alpha of .22 generates a squared error of 231.66. By repeating the example using different values for alpha you can determine which value results in the smallest error. To execute the program a second time start with step 4. Remember the values for steps 6 and 8 must be recomputed when you change the alpha value entered in step 7.

The values for alpha, S_{t-1}, T_{t-1} should be recorded for projecting the next periods forecast.

Forecasting When Alpha, S_{t-1}, and T_{t-1} are Known

When the values for alpha, S_{t-1}, and T_{t-1} are known forecasting is simple using exponential smoothing. The program given in the historical data section is used in this application.

The XYZ Company had sales of 496.26 in the first quarter of 1983. The alpha is .22, the smoothing factor (S_{t-1}) is 551.86, and the trend factor (T_{t-1}) is 3.61. The seasonal index for quarter 1 is 0.87 and is 0.94 for quarter 2.

Procedure	Press	Display
1. Clear calculator and mode registers; select two decimal places.	ON/c 2nd CLmode 2nd Fix 2	0.00
2. Press 2nd **Mode** until the "FIN" indicator is displayed.	2nd **Mode**	0.00
3. Enter exponential smoothing program.		
4. Clear mode registers and reset program.	2nd **CLmode** 2nd **RST**	0.00
5. Enter alpha.	.22 %i	0.22
6. Calculate and enter (1 − alpha)/alpha.	+/− + 1 ÷ RCL %i = PMT	3.55
7. Enter smoothing factor S_{t-1}.	551.86 PV	551.86
8. Enter trend factor T_{t-1}.	3.61 FV	3.61
9. Deseasonalize data.		
a. Enter 1983 first quarter sales.	496.26	496.26
b. Divide by seasonal index.	÷ 0.87	0.87
c. Calculate deseasonalized sales.	=	570.41

(continued)

(continued)

Procedure	Press	Display
10. Compute deseasonalized sales for 1983 second quarter.	[2nd] **RST** [R/S]	**569.11**
11. Multiply by seasonal index for second quarter to determine seasonalized sales.	[X] .94 [=]	**534.96**
12. Recall values to use for next quarter forecast.		
a. Seasonal smoothing factor S_{t-1}.	[RCL] [PV]	**555.94**
b. Trend factor T_{t-1}.	[RCL] [FV]	**3.71**
c. Alpha.	[RCL] [%i]	**0.22**

The projected seasonalized sales for the second quarter are $534.96. The values for alpha, S_{t-1}, and T_{t-1} should be recorded for next forecast.

A APPENDICES

RULE OF 78's INTEREST AMORTIZATION

total finance charge $= N \times PMT -$ loan amount

amount of interest in Kth payment

$$= \frac{N - K + 1}{\text{sum-of-the-years'-digits}} \times \text{total finance charge}$$

where:

$$\text{sum-of-the-years'-digits} = \frac{N (N + 1)}{2}$$

unearned interest rebate after K payments

$$= \frac{(N - K) (N - K + 1)}{N (N + 1)} \times \text{total finance charge}$$

amount of interest paid in K payments
$$= \text{total finance charge} - \text{interest rebate}$$

amount required to pay off loan after Kth payment
$$= \text{loan amount} + \text{amount of interest paid in K payments} - K \times PMT$$

where:

$N =$ total number of payments

$PMT =$ periodic payment amount

$K =$ number of current payment

PRESENT VALUE OF A STOCK WITH SUPERNORMAL GROWTH

Present value =

$$\frac{D_0 (1 + g_n)}{K_s - g_n} \ (1 + I)^{-N} \ + \ D_0 \left[\frac{1 - (1 + I)^{-N}}{I} \right]$$

where:

$D_0 =$ current dividend value

$N =$ number of supernormal growth periods

$K_s =$ expected rate of return

$g_n =$ normal growth rate

$I = \dfrac{(1 + K_s)}{1 + g_s} - 1$

$g_s =$ supernormal growth in decimal form

INVESTMENT RETURNS UNDER UNCERTAINTY

$$E(R) = \sum_{i=1}^{n} R_i P_i$$

$$\sigma_R = \sum_{i=1}^{n} (R_i - E(R))^2 P_i$$

where: $E(R)$ = expected value of project return

R_i = return for project if condition in period i exists

P_i = probability that condition in period i will occur

σ_R = standard deviation of expected value of return

STATISTICS

Standard deviation with N weighting

$$\sigma = \left[\frac{\Sigma x^2 - \dfrac{(\Sigma x)^2}{N}}{N} \right]^{1/2}$$

Standard deviation with N − 1 weighting

$$\sigma = \left[\frac{\Sigma x^2 - \dfrac{(\Sigma x)^2}{N}}{N-1} \right]^{1/2}$$

Variance $= \sigma^2$

Mean $= \bar{X} = \dfrac{(\Sigma x)}{N}$

Linear Regression

Slope (a) $= \dfrac{N(\Sigma xy) - (\Sigma y)(\Sigma x)}{N(\Sigma x^2) - (\Sigma x)^2}$

y-intercept (b) $= \dfrac{\Sigma y - a\Sigma x}{N}$

Correlation coefficient $= \dfrac{a\sigma_x}{\sigma_y}$

Standard error of the regression line

$$S_{y/x} = \left[(1 - r)^2 \; \sigma_y{}^2 \times N \times \frac{1}{N - 2} \right]^{1/2}$$

Standard error of slope

$$S_b = \frac{S_{y/x}}{\left[\sigma_x{}^2 \times N \right]^{1/2}}$$

where:

x = independent variable
$\overline{x}$ = mean or average of x values
N = number of elements in data set
σ = standard deviation
a = slope of regression line
b = y-intercept of regression line
r = correlation coefficient

PRESENT VALUE OF AN ANNUITY

$$PV = \left[1 + \frac{\%i}{100} \times K\right] \times PMT \left[\frac{1 - \left(1 + \frac{\%i}{100}\right)^{-N}}{\frac{\%i}{100}}\right]$$

$$+ FV\left[1 + \left(\frac{\%i}{100}\right)^{-N}\right]$$

where:

K = 0 if PMT occurs at the end of each payment period (ordinary annuity)

K = 1 if PMT occurs at the beginning of each payment period (annuity due).

Note: If the payment is positive, the interest is discounted. If the payment is negative, the interest is compounded.

SUM-OF-THE-YEARS'-DIGITS

For whole first year depreciation

$$D = (L + 1 - j)\left[\frac{2(C - S)}{L(L + 1)}\right]$$

For partial year depreciation

$$D = L(M)\left[\frac{(C - S)}{6(L)(L + 1)}\right]$$

For remaining year's depreciation

$$D = [12(L + 2 - j) - M]\left[\frac{(C - S)}{6(L)(L + 1)}\right]$$

where:

M = months of depreciation taken in first year

j = year number for calculation depreciation where j = 2, 3, ..., L, L + 1

L = depreciable life in years

C = cost

S = salvage value

STRAIGHT LINE DEPRECIATION

For whole first year:

$$\text{Dep/Yr} = \frac{\text{Cost - Salvage}}{\text{Life}}$$

First partial year depreciation:

$$D = \frac{\text{Months}}{12} (\text{Dep/Yr})$$

Last partial year depreciation:

$$D = \text{Dep/Yr} - \text{Depreciation for first partial year}$$

DECLINING BALANCE DEPRECIATION

For whole first year:

$$\text{Dep/Yr} = (\text{NBV}) \frac{(\text{DBF})}{L}$$

First year's partial depreciation:

$$D = \frac{M}{12} (\text{Cost}) \frac{\text{DBF}}{L}$$

where:

NBV = net book value
DBF = declining balance factor
M = number of months of depreciation
L = life of asset

BOND DURATION

$$\left[F(M + N_1)V^{N_1}(V^M) + \left(\frac{CV^N V^M}{i} \right) \right.$$

$$\left. \left((iM + 1)\left(\frac{1}{V^{N+1}} - 1 \right) - N_1 + 1 \right) + (M - 1)C \right] \div P$$

where:

F = bond redemption value

i = yield/100/(c/y)

c/y = coupons per year

M = partial coupon period as fraction

$M - 1$ = accrued interest period

N_1 = integer number of coupon periods

N = number of coupon periods, which may have a decimal portion

$V = \dfrac{1}{(1 + i)}$

P = settlement price

C = periodic coupon payment

CONVERTING APR TO EFF

$$EFF = \left[\left(1 + \frac{APR/100}{c/yr} \right)^{c/yr} - 1 \right] \times 100$$

where: c/yr = number of compounding periods per year for APR

CONVERTING EFF TO APR

$$APR = \left[\sqrt[c/yr]{1 + \frac{EFF}{100}} - 1 \right] \times c/yr \times 100$$

where: c/yr = number of compounding periods per year for APR

ECONOMIC ORDER QUANTITY

$$EOQ = \left[\frac{2 \times S \times OC}{SC} \right]^{1/2}$$

where:

EOQ = economic order (purchase) quantity
S = annual sales in units
OC = cost per order
SC = cost of carrying one unit in stock for one year

B APPENDICES

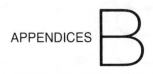
ERROR CONDITIONS

The display shows "Error" when overflow or underflow occurs or when an improper operation is requested. When this occurs, no entry from the keyboard except [OFF] is accepted until [ON/c] is pressed. You must then determine what caused the error and rekey the entry to avoid the problem.

The list of circumstances which cause *Error* to be displayed is as follows.

1. Number entry or calculation result (including in memories) is outside the range

     $-9.9999999 \times 10^{99}$ to -1×10^{-99},

    zero,

    or 1×10^{-99} to 9.9999999×10^{99}.

2. Square root of a negative number.

3. Dividing a number by zero.

4. Calculating **lnx** or [1/x] of 0.

5. Calculating **lnx** of a negative number.

6. Using an argument outside the range given in the Accuracy Information section of this appendix for the logarithmic functions.

7. Only one data point is used when calculating [σn-1].

8. When [σn] is calculated with no data points.

9. A data point is entered such that x is less than or equal to $\pm 1 \times 10^{-50}$ or x is greater than or equal to $\pm 1 \times 10^{50}$.

10. A series of data points is entered such that the sum of the squares exceeds the upper or lower limit of the calculator.

11. More than 99,999,999 data points are entered.

12. Data points are removed using [2nd] **Σ−** or [2nd] **Frq** [2nd] **Σ−** to the extent that there are zero or fewer data points.

13. Attempting linear regression calculations with less than two data points.

14. Attempting to calculate the y-intercept/slope for a vertical line in linear regression.

15. A percent change in which the old value is equal to zero is calculated.

16. The answer is less than or equal to -100% when %i is computed.

17. Entering a frequency of zero.

18. Entering a cash flow with a value greater than or equal to 1×10^8.

19. The calculation of N is attempted when PMT $\leq$ PV $\times$ %i.

20. Using [RCL], [STO], [SUM], or [EXC] for memories 0, 4-9 in statistical mode; 0, 6-9 in financial mode; or any memory that is not defined by the current partition in financial mode.

21. Pressing a function key unique to one mode while in another mode.

22. Pressing [R/S], [SST], or [2nd] **List** with no program steps.

23. Pressing any program function, including [2nd] **List**, when the calculator is not in the financial mode.

24. The calculation of financial unknowns is attempted before enough known variables are entered or is attempted when no solution exists.

25. The balance or interest is computed for a payment number less than 1.

26. The [APR►] or [◄EFF] key is used during computations in which the number of compounding periods per year is zero, the number of compounding periods per year is large, or %i is small.

APPENDICES B

ACCURACY INFORMATION

Each calculation produces an 11-digit result which is rounded to an 8-digit standard display. The 5/4 rounding technique used adds 1 to the least significant digit in the display if the next non-displayed digit is five or more. If this digit is less than five, no rounding occurs. In the absence of these extra digits, inaccurate results would frequently be displayed, such as

$1 \div 3 \times 3 = 0.9999999$

Because of rounding, the answer is given as 1, but is internally equal to 0.9999999999.

The higher order mathematical functions use iterative calculations. The cumulative error from these calculations in most cases is maintained beyond the 8-digit display so that no inaccuracy is displayed. Most calculations are accurate to ± 1 in the last displayed digit. There are a few instances in the solution of high order functions where display accuracy begins to deteriorate as the function approaches a discontinuous or undefined point. For example, when the y^x function has a y value that approaches 1 and an x value that is a very large positive or negative number.

The displayed result for 1.05^{-160} is accurate for all displayed digits, while 1.0000005^{-16000} is accurate to only five places.

The following gives the limits within which the display must be when calculating certain functions.

Function	Limit
ln x	$1 \times 10^{-99} \leqslant x < 1 \times 10^{100}$
e^x	$-227.95592 \leqslant x \leqslant 230.25850$

C APPENDICES

APPENDICES

IN CASE OF DIFFICULTY

In the event that you have difficulty with your calculator, the following instructions will help you to analyze the problem. You may be able to correct your calculator problem without returning the unit to a service facility. If the suggested remedies are not successful, contact the Consumer Relations Department by mail or telephone (refer to WARRANTY PERFORMANCE). Please describe in detail the symptoms of your calculator.

Symptom	Solution
Display is blank, shows erroneous results, flashes erratic numbers, or grows dim.	The battery may be discharged. Insert new batteries using the instructions in BATTERY REPLACEMENT.
Display shows erroneous results or "Error."	Review the operating instructions, including the error conditions appendix, to be certain that calculations were performed correctly.
Pressing LRN has no effect.	Calculator may not be in financial mode. Press 2nd Mode until "FIN" appears in the display.

If these procedures do not correct the difficulty, return the calculator prepaid and insured to the applicable Service Facility listed under Warranty Performance.

BATTERY REPLACEMENT

NOTE: The calculator cannot hold data in its user data memories or program memory when the batteries are removed or become discharged.

The calculator uses 2 of any of the following batteries for up to 750 hours of operation: Panasonic LR-44, Ray-O-Vac RW-82, Union Carbide (Eveready) A-76, or the equivalent. For up to 2000 hours of operation use Mallory 10L14, Union Carbide (Eveready) 357, Panasonic WL-14, Toshiba G-13, Ray-O-Vac RW-42, or the equivalent.

1. Turn the calculator off. Place a small screwdriver, paper clip, or other similar instrument into the slot and gently lift the battery cover.

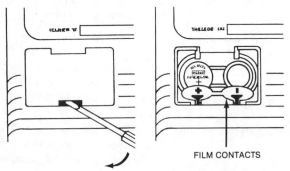

FILM CONTACTS

2. Remove the discharged batteries and install new ones as shown. Be careful not to crease the film contacts while installing the new batteries. Be sure the film contacts are positioned to lay on top of the batteries after the batteries are installed.
3. Replace the cover top edge first, then gently press until the bottom of the cover snaps into place.
4. Press ⌊ON/c⌋⌊ON/c⌋, ⌊2nd⌋ **CLmode**, ⌊2nd⌋ **CLmem**, ⌊2nd⌋ **CP**, and ⌊2nd⌋ **Fix** 8. The display then shows 0 and the calculator is ready to be used.

CAUTION: Do not incinerate the old batteries.

APPENDICES

CALCULATOR EXCHANGE CENTERS

If your calculator requires service, instead of returning the unit to your dealer or to a service facility for repair, you may elect to exchange the calculator for a factory-rebuilt calculator of the same model (or equivalent model specified by TI) by bringing the calculator in person to one of the exchange centers which have been established across the United States. No charge will be made for the exchange with proof-of-purchase during the first 90 days. The exchanged unit will be in warranty for the remainder of the original warranty period or for 6 months, whichever is longer. A handling fee will be charged for exchange after 90 days from the date of purchase. Out-of-warranty exchanges will be charged at the rates in effect at the time of the exchange. To determine if there is an exchange center in your locality, look for Texas Instruments Incorporated Exchange Center in the white pages of your telephone directory or look under the Calculator and Adding Machine heading in the yellow pages. Please call the exchange center for the availability of your model. Write the Consumer Relations Department for further details and the location of the nearest exchange center.

MAILING INSTRUCTIONS

Enclose a written explanation of the problem with your calculator. Be sure to include your name and return address.

Wrap your calculator in tissue or similar soft packing material and enclose it in a strong, crushproof mailing carton. If you use the original display box for mailing, it cannot be returned to you.

To protect your calculator from theft, do not write "calculator" on the outside of the package. Send your calculator to the appropriate address listed in WARRANTY PERFORMANCE.

Texas Instruments strongly recommends that you insure the product for value prior to mailing.

IF YOU NEED SERVICE INFORMATION

If you have questions concerning calculator repair, accessory purchase or the basic functions of your calculator, please write to:

Texas Instruments Consumer Relations
P.O. Box 53
Lubbock, Texas 79408

FOR TECHNICAL ASSISTANCE

For technical questions such as programming, specific calculator applications, etc., you can call (806) 747-3841. We regret that this is not a toll-free number, and we cannot accept collect calls. As an alternative, you can write to:

Texas Instruments Consumer Relations
P.O. Box 53
Lubbock, Texas 79408

California and Oregon: Consumers in California and Oregon may contact the following Texas Instruments offices for additional assistance or information.

Texas Instruments Consumer Service
831 South Douglas Street
El Segundo, California 90245
(213) 973-1803

Texas Instruments Consumer Service
6700 Southwest 105th St.
Kristin Square
Suite 110
Beaverton, Oregon 97005
(503) 643-6758

APPENDICES C

Because of the number of suggestions which come to Texas Instruments from many sources, containing both new and old ideas, Texas Instruments will consider such suggestions only if they are freely given to Texas Instruments. It is the policy of Texas Instruments to refuse to receive any suggestions in confidence. Therefore, if you wish to share your suggestions with Texas Instruments, or if you wish us to review any calculator program key sequence which you have developed, please include the following in your letter:

"All of the information forwarded herewith is presented to Texas Instruments on a nonconfidential, nonobligatory basis; no relationship, confidential or otherwise, expressed or implied, is established with Texas Instruments by this presentation. Texas Instruments may use, copyright, distribute, publish, reproduce, or dispose of the information in any way without compensation to me."

APPENDICES

ONE-YEAR LIMITED WARRANTY

THIS TEXAS INSTRUMENTS ELECTRONIC CALCULATOR WARRANTY EXTENDS TO THE ORIGINAL CONSUMER PURCHASER OF THE PRODUCT.

WARRANTY DURATION: This calculator is warranted to the original consumer purchaser for a period of one year from the original purchase date.

WARRANTY COVERAGE: This calculator is warranted against defective materials or workmanship. **THIS WARRANTY DOES NOT COVER BATTERIES AND IS VOID IF THE PRODUCT HAS BEEN DAMAGED BY ACCIDENT, UNREASONABLE USE, NEGLECT, IMPROPER SERVICE OR OTHER CAUSE NOT ARISING OUT OF DEFECTS IN MATERIAL OR WORKMANSHIP.**

WARRANTY DISCLAIMERS: ANY IMPLIED WARRANTIES ARISING OUT OF THIS SALE, INCLUDING BUT NOT LIMITED TO THE IMPLIED WARRANTIES OF MERCHANTABILITY AND FITNESS FOR A PARTICULAR PURPOSE, ARE LIMITED IN DURATION TO THE ABOVE ONE YEAR PERIOD. TEXAS INSTRUMENTS SHALL NOT BE LIABLE FOR LOSS OF USE OF THE CALCULATOR OR OTHER INCIDENTAL OR CONSEQUENTIAL COSTS, EXPENSES, OR DAMAGES INCURRED BY THE CONSUMER OR ANY OTHER USER. Some states do not allow the exclusion or limitation of implied warranties or consequential damages, so the above limitations or exclusions may not apply to you.

LEGAL REMEDIES: This warranty gives you specific legal rights, and you may also have other rights that vary from state to state.

WARRANTY PERFORMANCE: During the above one year warranty period your TI calculator will either be repaired or replaced with a reconditioned comparable model (at TI's option) when the product is returned, postage prepaid, to a Texas Instruments Service Facility listed below. In the event of replacement with a reconditioned model, the replacement product will continue the warranty of the original calculator or 6 months, whichever is longer. Other than the postage requirement, no charge will be made for such repair, adjustment, and/or replacement.

If the calculator is out of warranty, service rates in effect at the time of return will be charged. Please include information on the difficulty experienced with the calculator as well as return address information including name, address, city, state, and zip code. The shipment should be carefully packaged and adequately protected against shock and rough handling.

Texas Instruments Consumer Service Facilities

U. S. Residents:
Texas Instruments Service Facility
P.O. Box 2500
Lubbock, Texas 79408

Canadian customers only:
Geophysical Services Incorporated
41 Shelley Road
Richmond Hill, Ontario, Canada L4C5G4

NOTE: The P.O. Box number listed for the Lubbock Service facility is for United States parcel post shipments only. If you use another carrier, the street address is:

Texas Instruments Incorporated
2305 North University Avenue
Lubbock, TX 79415

D BIBLIOGRAPHY

BIBLIOGRAPHY  D

SELECTED BIBLIOGRAPHY

Brealey, Richard and Myers, Stewart. *Principles of Corporate Finance*. New York: McGraw-Hill, 1981.

Brueggeman, William B. and Stone, Leo D. *Real Estate Finance*. Seventh Edition. Homewood, Illinois: Richard D. Irwin, Inc., 1981.

Clark and Schkade. *Statistical Analysis for Administrative Decisions*. Second Edition. Cincinnati: South-Western Publishing Co., 1974.

Daniel, Wayne W. and Terrell, James C. *Business Statistics Basic Concepts and Methodology*. Second Edition. Dallas, Texas: Houghton Mifflin Company, 1979.

Greynolds, Elbert B. Jr., et al. *Business Analyst Guidebook*. Dallas: Texas Instruments, Inc., 1982.

Greynolds, Elbert B. Jr. and Stevens, Jan E. *Executive Calculator Guidebook*. Dallas: Texas Instruments, Inc., 1980.

Greynolds, Elbert B. Jr., Aronofsky, Julius S., and Frame, Robert J. *Financial Analysis Using Calculator: Time Value of Money*. New York: McGraw-Hill, 1980.

Horngren, Charles T. *Cost Accounting: A Managerial Emphasis*. Fifth Edition. Englewood Cliffs, New Jersey: Prentice-Hall, Inc., 1982.

Kieso, Donald E. and Weygandt, Jerry A. *Intermediate Accounting*. Third Edition. Santa Barbara, California: John Wiley and Sons, 1980.

"The Learning Curve as a Production Tool." *Harvard Business Review*, January-February 1954.

Van Horne, James C. *Financial Management and Policy*. Fifth Edition. Englewood Cliffs, New Jersey: Prentice-Hall, Inc., 1980.

Weston J. Fred and Brigham, Eugene F. *Managerial Finance*. Seventh Edition. Hinsdale, Illinois: The Dryden Press, 1981.

INDEX

INDEX E

(continued)

(continued)

NOTES

NOTES

NOTES

NOTES

NOTES

NOTES

NOTES

NOTES

NOTES

ADDENDUM

Please make the following changes to your manual.

Page 1-20

When removing data points, if only one data point or one pair of data points has been entered, remove it by pressing **CImode**.

Page 1-23

The procedure for calculating the variance of "x" data points with n and n-1 weighting should include pressing **[2nd] x^2** after **[x⇄y]**.

Page 1-33

Steps 1 and 2 should be reversed to read as follows.

Procedure	Press	Display
1. Press **[2nd] [Mode]** until the "FIN" indicator is displayed.	**[2nd] [Mode]**	**0.00**
2. Clear calculator and program; select two decimal places.	**[ON/C] [2nd] [CP]** **[2nd] [Fix] 2**	**0.00**

Page 2-11

In the first time-line diagram, the value for FV should be $1.12682503.

Page 2-12

The last sentence on the page should read as follows.

For more information about annual percentage rates and annual effective rates, see the application entitled "Finding Interest Rate (Yield) when Buyer Pays Points" in chapter 5 and "Applications with a Series of Variable Deposits, Solving for Future Value" in chapter 9. Also see appendix A for the formulas used in these applications.

Page 5-43

The display in step 5 should be 1.20.

Page 11-15

The display in step 13 should be 1139633.70.

Page A-2

The formula for standard deviation of expected value of return for Investment Returns Under Uncertainty should be as follows.

$$\sigma_R = \left[\sum_{i=1}^{n} (R_i - E(R))^2 P_i \right]^{1/2}$$

Page C-2

The Mallory 10L14 battery has been replaced by Mallory D357.